D0001388

What Readers Are Saying About
Better Than
Espresso

"Julie's biblical insights, inspiring stories, and humorous examples *in Better Than Espresso* will help you renew your mind and shut out those nagging negative thoughts. Alongside the Bible, this devotional will help you move forward, stay focused on the truth, and become fixated not on the lies you tend to tell yourself, but on the truth of who you are in the eyes of your fully capable, loving Creator. Don't start your morning without it!"

Cindi McMenamin, National Speaker, Bible teacher, and author of several books, including *When Women Walk Alone, When A Woman Overcomes Life's Hurts,* and *God's Whispers to a Woman's Heart.*

"Julie's transparency comes through in such a real way, you feel like you're across the table having a conversation over a cup of coffee. Julie's vulnerability helps us understand she's been where we've been. Looking at the emotions we experience from time to time – guilt, shame, fear, lack of purpose – through a biblical filter always provides greater peace and clarity. Julie guides us to do just that: to reflect on our situations in light of God's truth – and what a perfect time in history to have this as a resource!"

Lisa T. Grimes, Managing Director, Habergeon LLC, Board Chair, Knowing God Ministries, Co-author, *Remember Who YOU Are,* and *25 Days of Christmas for Your Heart,* and *Home.*

Better than Espresso is the perfect addition to your personal devotion library! Julie's personal stories and that of her friends are shared with a beautiful authenticity that is rare. They are laced with humor, candor, and hope. By reading them, you will find that regardless of your circumstances, God is faithful! You will laugh, cry, and go away with new ways to reframe your circumstances with beautiful scripture. So, grab your cup of coffee, sit down and experience a little time with Julie that is **Better than Espresso!**

Linda Johns, Specializing in Relational Trauma, Professional Certified Life Coach ,Certified Partner Coach (APSATS), Instructor Christian Life Coach, Certified Recovery Coach.

"Julie has an amazing way of speaking directly into the heart of the challenges women face. Her application of the timeless truths in Scripture - turning them into 'sticky quotes' is revolutionary in empowering us to defeat our fears and insecurities!"

Tara Furman, Founder and President of Knowing God Ministries, Author of *Knowing God, Created for Purpose,* and *The 7 Day Challenge; Jumpstart your Marriage in a Week.*

"Julie has such a beautiful way of talking real life issues, dignifying those issues and ultimately bringing them into Biblical wisdom. Through *Better Than Espresso* Julie gets to the core of a woman's heart. In her writing she helps her reader identify what's been holding her captive and then points herto reflection and Biblical truth. What a great way to start your day, with a cup of coffee, time in the Word and *Better Than Espresso.*"

Rachel Cherie Baker, Director of Women's Ministry, Life-Point Church Nevada, author of *Deconstructed Bible Study Guide* and *Deconstructing Esther.*

"I was laughing and crying as I read Julie's devotional, *Better than Espresso!* Her practical sayings from God's Word speak directly to the female experience! She says them in a way that makes them stick! I will be using this awesome devotional as I soak in His presence, mentor women, and lead my own ministry. Thank you Julie for placing my mindset in perspective so I can walk in truth and confidence again."

Roxanna Grimes, Co-Founder of The Relationship Warehouse, Author of *Pearl*, Trained Counselor.

Better Than
Espresso

JULIE PEARSON

Amazon Publishing

Seattle, Washington

Copyright © 2020 by Julie Pearson

Unless otherwise indicated, all Scripture quotations are from the Holy Bible New International Version, © 1973, 1978, 1984, 2011 by Biblica, Inc.
Verses marked ESV are taken from the ESV® Bible (the Holy bible, English Standard Version®). Copyright © 2001 by Crossway, a publishing ministry of Good News Publishers.
NKJV are taken from the New King James Version, © 1982 by Thomas Nelson, Inc.
Verses marked NLT are taken from the Holy Bible, New Living Translation, copyright ©1996. Tyndale House Publishers, Inc. Wheaton, IL 60189.
Verses marked MSG are taken from The Message. Copyright © by Eugene H. Peterson 1993, 1994, 1995, 1996, 2000, 2001, 2002. Tyndale House Publishers.
Italicized text in Scripture quotations indicate author's emphasis.

All rights reserved. No part of this publication may be reproduced, distributed or transmitted in any form or by any means, including photocopying, recording, or other electronic or mechanical methods, without the prior written permission of the publisher, except in the case of brief quotations embodied in critical reviews and certain other noncommercial uses permitted by copyright law. For permission requests, write to the publisher, addressed "Attention: Permissions Coordinator," at the address below.

Julie Pearson/Amazon Publishing
Seattle, Washington
Book Layout ©2017 BookDesignTemplates.com
Better Than Espresso/ Julie Pearson
Cover by: Christina Suarez
ISBN 978-0-578-68943-2

Contents

Part 3: When the Burden of Hurt, Pain, and Shame Bind You

Part 4: When You Feel Lost in Your Purpose and Direction

Part 5: When Your Identity is Threatened

Part 6: When You're Changed by God's Character

To my beautiful kids Brianna, Cole, and Ashlyn.
I pray you grow in faith and Godly confidence
throughout your journey of life.

The Power of a "Sticky Quote"

H ave you ever sat through a movie and heard a quote that forever stuck in your mind? Maybe it moved you emotionally or sparked a ray of hope. Some movies leave a great legacy because of a famous line. Here are a few famous one-liners that have stuck in our minds throughout the generations.

"I'm going to make him an offer he can't refuse." (*The Godfather*, 1972)

"Here's looking at you, kid." (*Casablanca*, 1942)

"May the force be with you." (*Star Wars*, 1977)

"There's no place like home." (*The Wizard of Oz*, 1939)

"You had me at hello." (*Jerry Maguire*, 1996)

I love quotes, especially ones that offer hope and inspiration. They have the ability to turn a bad day into a new day, forge us forward, teach us a valuable lesson, and reframe a negative thought into a positive one. Over the years, I have created and journaled my own quotes, either from an inspiring message or a passage of Scripture I studied.

I'm also a coffee lover. There is nothing like awakening to the strong smell of a brewing pot of coffee. A morning cup of coffee is awesome, but words of wisdom are what help our minds blossom. Words have the power to shape our thoughts, and our thoughts set the trajectory of our lives. Our thoughts produce the winning mindsets we need first thing in the morning to start our day off strong, like my favorite brew of coffee.

I wrote this devotional after breaking out of a tough season of life in which lies and shame were whirling around my mind like a tornado. I was moving steadily in the fast track and then suddenly, red lights appeared ahead, causing me to screech to a complete halt. I was not moving forward anymore. In fact, I wasn't moving *anywhere*. As I tried to pick myself up, I found my mind became my enemy. It started reminding me of my not-so-pleasant past, filling me with false narratives that I started to believe. Bullying words, failures, and self-doubt impeded my mind. It was obvious I was stuck in the mud and it became very difficult to pull myself out. My morning moments were the hardest. I needed something more than my cup of coffee to fill me, to grasp onto; something to keep me moving, mindful, and motivated. Reading my Bible, journaling, and seeking counsel were obvious helps. However, I needed something my eyes could fixate on to repeat daily positive messages and destroy the lies cemented in my mind. My "Sticky Quotes" started to become another anchor, offering me the hope and eternal perspective I needed. When life gets messy and my thoughts get muddy, my sticky quotes have come to my rescue (coffee would sometimes make it better too). I look straight into my mirror, with my morning messy face glaring back at me, and with conviction and commitment recite my "sticky quote." Repeating each one daily provided the cognitive therapy my soul desperately needed. We have probably all heard the saying, *What gets recited, gets repeated.*

If you find yourself stuck from lies and negative beliefs swirling around in your mind, what helps you? Do inspirational quotes stir your soul like they do mine? How do *you* respond when you read or hear a poignant quote and better yet, a passage of life-changing Scripture? Do you find that it instills hope in you and positively impacts your day? That's what I hope this devotional will do for you as you sit with your morning coffee to pause and reflect on faithful portions of Scripture and truth.

These inspirational spiritual messages – read first thing every morning -- will prayerfully renew your mind and keep you from feeling stuck. This book is a compilation of my sticky quotes to move and motivate you, along with an inspiring passage of Scripture and a background or personal story related to each quote. It is my hope and prayer that you will grow in your faith, endurance, and personal development as you ponder the daily quote, start reciting it, and eventually, live it. I encourage you to reflect on the questions at the end of each chapter and journal your thoughts. That's where the application and personal development happen. You are not alone with these battling emotions: the grip of fear, the loss of courage and confidence, the shame that binds your heart, and a lack of purpose and direction. These are all feelings I have struggled with, too, so I share personal stories, illustrations, and Scripture that have helped put my mind and emotions at ease. Whether you are a woman of faith or not, I hope to inspire you to a greater hope found in the Savior of this world, Jesus Christ.

Here's another exciting part. If you go to my book page https://juliepearson.org/book/ subscribe, you will receive a free downloadable of a beautifully decorated full-color print of a sticky quote. I have also created non-adhesive mirror decals of these sticky quotes. You can place them on your mirror and with your morning face, recite it, repeat it, and start your day off right! **Don't stay stuck in the mud! Grab your cup of coffee and get stuck in the sticky quote.**

Part 1

When Fear is Gripping You

Day 1

There is Purpose in
My Pause

Come and see what the LORD has done, He makes
wars cease
to the ends of the earth. He says, "Be still, and know
that I am God;
I will be exalted among the nations, I will be exalted
in the earth." The LORD Almighty is with us; the
God of Jacob is our fortress.
(Psalm 46: 8-11)

Who would have guessed we would ever endure such a fearful and alarming pandemic? As I write this, our world has come to a screeching halt due to the Coronavirus outbreak (now and forever known as COVID-19). Stocks are diving, travel is minimized, kids are no longer in school, and families are quarantined in their homes. Our generations have never seen anything quite like this before. People are dying as this virus is sweeping through every nation in the world. It's eerie to see streets in New York City empty and the mandated lockdowns forcing our busy world into isolation. Life is on pause, and the scary thing is we don't know how long it will last. Humans, even the brightest in the world, have lost a sense of control. Hence, fear and panic has penetrated the human soul like a nail injected into a tire. Moment by moment we become flattened by fear, as food and supplies appear depleted. Panic is increasing as pressure builds in the media. People are hoarding toilet paper and paper goods, allowing scarcity to drum up more fear. I am sure you are wondering like me, *Why the craze over toilet paper?* Humanity doesn't make sense sometimes. Rummaging through the grocery stores and seeing empty shelves is a sure sign – *people are panicked, fearful, anxious about the future, and out of control!*

Pauses are not comfortable for any of us, especially as a 21st century productive person. Would you agree our culture is not accustomed to silence and stillness? We like the fast pace, it gives us a certain thrill. Staying busy working long strenuous hours and weekends jammed packed running from the soccer field to the baseball field, keeps us pre-occupied and in control. It seems we prefer busyness rather than enjoying the pleasures of life- spending quality time with family, playing silly games, a leisure walk through the park, sit down dinners, and a visit with a sick friend. Busyness gives our egos a boost, the busier we are and the more we produce, the worthier we feel. Now I don't condemn productivity, I am the master at setting goals and achieving all I can. I also know God despises laziness. "Lazy hands make for poverty, but diligent hands bring wealth" (Proverbs 10:4). But I think today's culture disallows rest and pause because stillness makes us feel uncomfortable. It invites soul searching and quite frankly, who enjoys that! Most of us would rather scurry with busyness than attend to our souls. The problem is, if we don't learn to value our pauses and attend to our souls, it's easy to ignore the signs of an unhealthy and unbalanced life. This is when life really falls apart; a phone call from your doctor with a diagnosis that could have been prevented. So perhaps the pause is to remind us, a balanced life is more precious than a busy chaotic life.

Honestly, my old self would probably feel more panicked and anxious experiencing this global crisis of pause. But I believe God prepared me emotionally for this crisis. I have recently been through a personal pause questioning my purpose and where my future was leading me. I feared the unknown. False narratives ravaging through my mind felt like my life was stuck in never-ending, congested traffic; confined, halted, with absolutely no movement and momentum. I was interrupted by these false beliefs and it was extremely uncomfortable for a girl who likes to move forward, stay busy, and produce. Fear, anxiety, and panic swept my emotions. It felt like I was in a bad snow storm which kept me more and more isolated, not healthy for any soul. I realized I could not allow fear and anxiety continue to feed my soul. I used this time of pause to improve my mindfulness, release and heal from scenarios feeding my negative emotions. Guided meditations (found on You Tube) allowed my soul and mind to be still and know "that He is God."

Be Still

Psalm 46 is a beautiful scripture passage and a good reminder that God comforts us when things look threatening and out of control. It encourages us to place our hope and trust in Him, not in the unpredictable world. He is much bigger than our current pandemic~ He is preparing a greater purpose behind the world's pause. What if we were to rely on this perspective? Might we move in greater faith than crazy fear? God uses times of crisis to teach us lessons, remind us who is in control and "be still and know that I am God." He ceases wars, He is the Lord almighty. Isn't this enough for us to be reassured He is our refuge, our strength, our prince of peace even in times of Pandemic and crisis?

How have you seen God be your refuge and strength, an ever-present help in times of fear and trouble? If you are a person who places your hope and trust in our Lord almighty, I am positive you can see places in your life where God showed up and gave you more strength than you had for yourself. That's who the God of this world is: He extends peace beyond human understanding, in spite of panic and pandemic. Is this the message of purpose behind our global pause? *A God of peace in the panic.* I can imagine the chaos taking place in our medical facilities as doctors scramble to find resolutions beyond their human capacity. I think God is preparing to reveal his sovereignty, especially in the medical field as our global crisis continues. I can't wait to hear the stories, aren't you curious too? We serve a God who desires ALL of humanity to know Him and sometimes it takes a crisis to remind us of His compassion.

I see the greater purpose in my own pause and I hope you can too. I have a better self-awareness of who I am and what God has given me. He is helping me work through my fears, hurt, pain, and areas of weakness. He is giving me greater strength, so I can be used by Him in greater ways. I have more compassion for the hurting, which is the greater lesson because I traditionally score low on compassion and mercy on personality tests. Yes, my pause has been painful and uncomfortable at times, but as I see the purpose unveiling, it changes my perspective. God is working for me, not against me. I hope you too can gain a healthier perspective and evaluate God's purpose in your pause.

I am confident there is greater purpose in our global pause. Many lessons are being learned and shaped. We are regrouping globally. We are more united than ever, learning newer and greater strategies to prevent another likely pandemic. Becoming more like Jesus, compassionate for the sick, dying, and those in need. Reminding us we are not in control, but there is a greater prince of peace who is. The God of Jacob has been, and is, and will always be our refuge and strength in times of fear, panic, worry, and trouble.

God's refuge is *Better Than Espresso*

.

Reflecting on Your Purpose in the Pause

❖ How has the Coronavirus global pandemic affected you?

❖ Think about other "pauses" that have happened in your life. How did you react to them? Did it cause fear and anxiety for you?

❖ What do you think is the greater purpose behind your pauses?

❖ If you would like guidance on learning to "Be still and know that I am God" to ease your anxiety and fear, I would like to recommend an exercise of guided meditation. Go to You Tube and search "Christian guided meditation." You will find calming exercises to remind you of how the Lord Almighty has control over your life.

Day 2

God is My Strength, He is Bigger Than My Failure

Don't panic. I'm with you.
There's no need to fear for I'm your God.
I'll give you strength. I'll help you.
I'll hold you steady, keep a firm grip on you.
(Isaiah 41:9-10 MSG)

It was the dreaded moment of preparing for the SAT test. It was my daughter's Junior Year of high school. I received tons of mailings trying to sell me on prep courses, so I did what any ultra-prepared, concerned mom would do. I enrolled her into a one-day prep course. I wanted to equip her as much as possible because if she was anything like me, I stunk at taking standardized tests.

A month after her prep course, we received her practice test scores in the mail. *Ouch!* The first thing that caught my eye was the **BIG FAT RED MARKS** on her writing sample. My palms immediately got clammy. As I anxiously stared at her red marks, they reminded me of my own red marks (failing a similar test), holding me hostage to the fear of failure for many years. I was hesitant to show her the results. I didn't want her to feel defeated by this test. *Would she perceive herself as a failure as I had years ago?* I probably was making a bigger deal about this practice test than I should have. I guess this is what *fear of failure* does to us. It can cause us to act neurotic, even disabled by it. Perhaps it's because we can allow our failure to define who we are.

Can you identify with my neurosis? Is there a failure you have not moved past, and it's still locked and loaded on your weight-baring chest? Has it caused you to be afraid of trying again? How have you allowed it to define you? I'm still working on not allowing my own red marks to define and fear me. Our red marks are a perfect scenario for the enemy to destroy our identity and prevent us from moving forward. A disruptive relationship with a child or marriage may send the message, *You failed in this meaningful relationship and now you are no longer worthy of love.* Wow, look how damaging failure can look in our lives if we don't learn to reframe it. It alludes to the hidden message of inadequacy prompting more fear to reside in our hearts and minds.

Everyone will experience failure at one time or another. How we learn from our failure (instead of dwell and become paralyzed by it) is important. The mindset we develop after significant failures is what really matters. Our mindset will either influence positively or negatively the important things in life, our relationships, and even our mental health. Aren't you amazed by athletic teams that bounce back after significant defeats? I love to watch comebacks from people who have experienced great failures and defeats. They are people to follow and learn from. But why do some recover, while others do not? I believe it has to do with strength and strategy. One good strategy is to realize our failures are not forever, they are temporary.

The red marks on my daughter's test were rectifiable. With hard work and effort, she could learn from her mistakes and get better. It seemed like a daunting task for her, but as you and I learn to work through our failures, we gain more empowerment for the next one. Furthermore, as Isaiah 41:9-10 instructs: don't panic when the enemy of defeat rages inside. These are the moments when we must replace our temporary red marks about how we've performed with the permanent red marks (of Jesus' blood) sacrificed for us on the cross. Those red marks undoubtedly help us reframe the disruption of defeat. They allow us to reach into the depth of our soul and know full well, *God is our strength, He is bigger than any failure we encounter.*

Strength in Failure

During the time of Isaiah, God's people were feeling threatened by their enemies. The neighboring powers were so much greater than their own. But God spoke tenderly to His people, saying "Fear not. I will give you the strength you need, I'll keep you steady with My firm grip on you." In that time of history, Israel felt like the worm, the weaker vessel. They were surrounded by stronger enemies who tried to destroy their identity, just like our enemy who focuses on our failures. I'm sure you, at some time, have identified with the Israelites, feeling weak, depleted of all your human strength. But God is trying to convince His people not to lean on themselves to manage their upsets, but to lean on Him. In time, we will see how God's strength becomes a "threshing" instrument. A thresher is used by a farmer to make his work more efficient, producing more seed and grain from the crops. How awesome it is that as we tap into God's strength, the thresher keeps us healthy and efficient, instead of gripped by fear.

I admit it's difficult not to fear when we are experiencing huge defeats. It's in our human nature to try to control our lives. When mistakes and failures creep into the picture, we usually go into self-preservation mode, sometimes even crawl into our caves. A common problem though, is that when we isolate, it deters us from learning the valuable lesson. Perhaps there is some character trait God is trying to mold, or a message God is trying to reveal to us. Ultimately, Christ came to erase our red marks (failures) and exchange them for His permanent ones. His sacrificed red marks empower us to put our boots on the ground, fight, and live victoriously in Him. There is often a larger opportunity ahead if we are diligent learners and fighters in Christ. As we learn to reframe our failures as temporary and not define our lives by them, we seek the preeminent opportunity God is preparing ahead. This, my friend, will prevent us from fearing failure, and instigate the fight to move forward.

God's Strength is *Better Than Espresso*

Reflecting on Your Fear of Failure

❖ What failure stands out the most in your life?

❖ How has that failure caused you fear in the past?

❖ Think about red marks written with a dry erase pen on a white board. As they can easily be erased, your "red marks" can be easily erased too, because they are temporary, not permanent. How does this visual encourage you to fight your failures, instead of fear them?

❖ Write a prayer to God in the space below, asking Him to exchange your "red marks" for His. (This exchange is the catalyst to helping you fight your fear of failure.) I'm so glad God erases my failures, aren't you?

Day 3

Worry Exhausts,
Wisdom Energizes

*"Come to me, all who labor and are heavy laden,
and I will give you rest. Take my yoke upon you,
and learn from me, for I am gentle and lowly in
heart, and you will find rest for your souls. For
my yoke is easy, and my burden is light."*
(Matthew 11:28-30 ESV)

It's the middle of the night. I'm tossing and turning, my stomach twisted in knots. Anxiety has struck again, and my mind is racing with negative thoughts compromising my needed sleep. Does this sound familiar?

If you are a mom, no matter the ages of your kids, can you agree that worry is a common thread? I come from a long lineage of worriers and I have inherited this characteristic quite well.

Your worries for your children may look different than mine. We tend to remember the struggles, hardships, and disappointments of our own past and those become the worries we have about our own children. I worry about my kids' academics, future careers, their safety, and if they are going to be bullied at school. Excelling at academics did not come naturally for me. I had to study extra hard to achieve good grades. I was never diagnosed with a learning disability, but I knew I had a deficiency somewhere in my ability to process. Once my kids started school, I worried about their academic successes. I didn't want them to struggle like I did!

I think a common worry we all have as moms is our kids' safety. Our saving grace as 21st Century moms is we have tracking devices on our phones, so we have the ability to know the whereabouts of our children, unlike the moms who worried about us. But still, our children's safety is a concern no matter how sophisticated our technology becomes. In fact, a couple weeks ago my son spent the night at a friend's house and he was supposed to meet us at the soccer fields the next morning for his game. My husband and I approached the field with his coach and teammates asking for Cole's whereabouts. "What? Where is my son? He should be here!" Panic struck my heart, but then we calmly tracked our son on our phones and his location was revealed. (Can you believe my son overslept, almost causing a heart attack for his mother?)

Do you worry about your child's social life at school? I was bullied in Jr. High, so I understand the damage of bullying. I can't even imagine if I was bullied as a child in today's world with social media. The pressures our children encounter are much greater, and enough to send worry and fear down our spines.

Whether you're a mom or not, worry and anxiety creeps into our souls. Some more than others. The problem with so much worry is it wearies our burdened souls. Our intense uncertainty can burden those around us as well. I know my kids can sense my concern and sometimes it can cause them to become anxious. There is nothing good that comes from anxiety. Numerous studies show how anxiety impacts our physical and mental health. Our culture is experiencing an epidemic with anxiety, causing more and more young people to take their own lives. Something needs to happen to stop these terrifying statistics.

Help in our Worry

There is help in our worry. Whether you consider yourself a follower of Jesus or not, I'm certain you have heard of Him; He has the answers for us if we will just heed His advice. He gently commands us to come to Him. He knows the pressures of the world and Jesus is the *only* One who will give us rest. In Matthew 11:29, He used the analogy of a yoke to make His point. A yoke is a wooden harness attached to a pair of oxen to get the animals to work together to tread the fields. We are like oxen. There is a yoke that we use to steer, direct, and control our lives. For many of us, our yoke is the pleasures and directions we receive from the world. However, Jesus confidently stated that if we replace our yoke with His, we experience true rest. I desire rest from my burdens, don't you? Perhaps you and I should give Jesus' yoke a try.

Scripture tells me to harness my yoke with Jesus, but at times I resist. The world's offerings are often more enticing. But, I know Jesus got it right. Wealth, honor and power are fruitless cares compared to His ways and His wisdom. He also knows the burden of guilt when I choose to go my own way. Jesus doesn't want to force me into obedience of exchanging my yoke, because He knows it will still be a burden if it's forced. Jesus invites me, without force, to take His yoke and learn from Him. He is waiting with anticipation to show me how my life will be changed with more rest, ease, and energy instead of weariness in my worry.

Are you, too, burdened by anxiety and worry? What would it look like to exchange your yoke with His? When anxiety strikes, stop immediately. Recite and repeat several times, *"Come to me, I will give you rest."* Visualize Jesus' hand on your nervous belly, exchanging your anxious energy for His essential energy. The moment I sense worry and anxiety permeating my mind, I stop, pray, and if I have a few minutes, I open my Bible and journal my anxious heart to God. As a result, I am equipped with more wisdom and I often meet rest and calmness immediately. Wouldn't you agree that our exhaustion from our worry is because we want control and won't let Jesus be our yoke?

As you and I learn to transfer our overworked worry into the lap of Jesus, something miraculously happens. Suddenly we become women not exhausted by worry but eased by rest.

> **We become Women not exhausted by worry but eased by rest.**

Your worried finances won't keep you up at night. That child you're concerned for is in better hands. You are leading with less anxiety and more ambition because you chose to exchange your yolk. This rest wouldn't have been offered if it wasn't true. *His yoke is easy, and His burden is light.*

His yoke of rest is *Better Than Espresso*

Reflecting on Your Worry

❖ What is a worry that most burdens you in this very moment? What keeps you from using Jesus' yoke? (Are you afraid to give up control? Do you doubt Jesus' claim that his yoke is easy and the burden light?) Journal your answer in the space below.

❖ Spend a few moments of solitude. Grab your ipad, phone, or computer and listen to some spiritual meditation music on YouTube. (Search *soaking music* and you will find several options.) Close your eyes, breathe deeply, and invite the Holy Spirit into your heart. Recite and repeat God's promising words as you sit and quiet your soul.

- "Come to me, and I will give you rest." (Mathew 11:28)
- The peace of God, which transcends all understanding, will guard my mind and heart. (Philippians 4:7)
- He restores my soul and guides me along the right path. (Psalm 23:3)
- Cast all my anxiety on him, because He cares for me. (1 Peter 5:7)
- Anxiety weighs down my heart, but a kind word cheers it up. (Proverbs 12:25)
- God is for me, not against me. (Romans 8:31)

Wasn't that worth it to quiet your worried soul?

Day 4

Fear Asks: *What if it Doesn't Work?* Faith Asks: *What if it Does Work?*

For I am the LORD your God who takes hold of your right hand and says to you, Do not fear; I will help you.
(Isaiah 41:13)

Fear holds us hostage. It stops us and gets in our way. One of the guest speakers at my ministry conference presented an amazing personal testimony about what our lives look like if we allow fear to get in the way. If she allowed fear to stop her from ministering to oppressed children on the streets, a young 8-year-old boy would have never had the chance for healing and escaping a horrific situation. The story was difficult to receive, but it resonated with me and provided a great visual of what happens if we allow fear to reign more than our faith.

I remember when God gave me an assignment, but I kept making excuses because I was afraid. My heart pounded, it felt like it was coming out of my chest. Thoughts like *What if it doesn't work?* held me hostage. When we find ourselves battling this question, fear has usually found its way into the crevices of our thoughts. A crevice is a narrow opening, a fissure, especially in a rock. Fear likes the crevice because it disguises itself little by little. It's not one big moment that causes us to stop in fear, it's little experiences that fester and grow. They seep into the crevices of our minds until one day, fear has laid its damaging foundation, leaving us more to restore.

Has there been an assignment in your life in which your intervention could bring more hope than fear and trepidation? What did you do with that assignment? Are you still contemplating it because you are blocked by fear, or did you erase fear with faith? It's a shame when opportunities are missed because our fear gets in the way.

Faith Counters Fear

Faith counters fear and the words of Jesus are a great example. As we study His miracles, there is usually a common thread. On more than one occasion Jesus expressed, "because of your great faith, you are healed." Jesus enjoys watching us display faith over fear. He wants to see us exercise faith *more* than fear. Why? Because faith welcomes Him. Fear, however, places confidence in our own fallible hands. I know my confidence is nothing compared to what Jesus can offer me. So why do I give more energy to fear?

It's amazing how many times we see the words *fear not* in the Bible. Google search says it is mentioned 365 times. Is it no coincidence there is one *fear not* for every day of the year.

I love the visual of God holding up our right hand as He graciously proclaims: "Do not fear, I will help you." All through His Word are examples of how He rescued those in need, provided resources when there were none. He even turned "desert into pools of water, and the parched ground into spring" (Isaiah 41:18). What makes us think God can't help us after reading verses like that?

You and I can't go wrong with more faith and less fear; anxiety decreases, dreams are accomplished, lives are changed. Why is this a difficult truth to embrace? Is it because fear of what we know is easier than jumping into the pool of the unknown? Probably so. Jumping into the unfamiliar is like jumping into a pool of cold, fresh water on a brisk day. Faith requires us to jump in and step out into the uncomfortable; resist the repeated no's during the job search, face another relationship despite previous betrayal, and place our confidence in something bigger than ourselves. As I plunge into my fear little by little, I see myself accomplishing more than I thought I could. I help people become better when I don't let fear get in the way. I'm so glad fear didn't stop the guest speaker either. That 8-year- old boy deserved to be rescued and given a life of hope.

If fear has reigned more than faith, take a step of courage and ask yourself, *What if it does work?* Lean into what a life of faith looks like versus a life of fear. I am absolutely positive the trajectory of your life will change for the better because you chose faith over fear. That is worth celebrating, my friend.

Faith rather than fear is *Better Than Espresso*

Reflecting on Fear

❖ What are you yearning to do, yet you find yourself thinking *What if it doesn't work?*

❖ What exactly are you afraid of?

❖ What would the situation look like if you said, "What if it *does* work?" Mark all that apply.

My children will benefit: _____

I would gain more confidence: _____

Someone's life will be changed: _____

My relationship will be restored: _____

I will gain a new skill: _____

My finances will be better: _____

Part 2

When You Lack Courage, Confidence, and Perseverance

Day 5

Life Will Knock Me Down, But I Have a Choice to Get Back Up

"Have I not commanded you? Be strong and courageous. Do not be afraid; do not be discouraged, for the Lord your God will be with you wherever you go."
(Joshua 1:9)

One of my favorite movies is *The Karate Kid.* The original 1984 film was the best, but I enjoyed all the sequels, especially the later ones I watched with my children. Not only is *Karate Kid* one of my favorites, but also all the *Rocky* movies. I guess you could say I love watching a good fight in which the underdog gets back on his feet.

My husband and I have three athletic children. I spend many hours watching my kids excel in their sports. My youngest daughter is a competing gymnast. As with any sport, there is plenty of perseverance and determination needed for her to succeed as an athlete. I remember a meet where she was performing like the Karate Kid. Nothing she did was going in her favor. It was time to perform her first event, the balance beam. Her poise was beautiful, and her spirit was confident. As she launched into her first handstand, her hands made it on the beam but to her dismay, her feet slipped off the beam and she fell. Surprise and shock set in, but she got up and tried again. Another try, but again her feet brushed off the side of the beam. She got back up and tried again. A third, fourth and fifth attempt. Finally, after the sixth attempt, her feet decided to land on the beam. She sadly finished her routine and her face revealed it all. She was knocked down by her performance and felt despair, discouragement, and failure.

Have you ever felt like that? Knocked down by life and it's so difficult to get back up? Maybe it's been more than just one missed handstand. Maybe for you it has been a series of knock downs. I can imagine how difficult it was for my daughter to get back up on the beam after multiple knock downs and finish her routine. It was heart-wrenching to watch!!

Why is it so difficult to make the choice to get back up again? We are afraid to get back up because we can't stand the thought of losing again. We don't want to look like a failure in front of everyone. It's humbling to get knocked down repeatedly. I remember thinking these same thoughts as I watched *The Karate Kid* for the first time. I was so afraid for Daniel when he was challenged to fight the bigger, stronger fighter. I was not only afraid for his safety, but I was afraid for his dignity after he was knocked down several times. I saw his will to fight as an encouragement for us to get back up again.

It Takes Courage

It requires courage to get back up and keep going when results don't seem promising. One of the greatest role models of courage in the Bible is Joshua. He was used by God to fulfill the call of Moses and lead the Israelites into the Promised Land. There was one more barrier the Israelites had to overcome – cross the Jordan River and then they would finally enter God's country. But there was one problem. Joshua didn't have any bridge or boat to cross over the rushing waters. He would also have to fight the people on the other side; they were the enemies. God commanded Joshua to cross over, "Be strong and courageous, for the Lord your God will be with you." The only weapon Joshua possessed was his weapon of faith. There was nobody to rely on, no arsenal to prepare for battle, no resources to comfort his large task of crossing over. He just had to believe and walk in courage.

Ouch. This is a difficult task .... Just believe. You probably have had these words spoken over you from a friend who is trying to encourage you in your beaten-down moments. I have too. But when you're on the floor, with no strength or confidence to get back up, and your enemy is intimidating you, that takes more courage than any human can muster up. I knew my daughter could not finish her disastrous routine by herself. The only thing I could do in that moment was pray that God would give her the courage to press on until the end. Thankfully, He did.

Life may have knocked you down, but tap into your tenacity and work your way off the ground. Start with one successful move, like make a phone call or learn something new. This is courage; you're fighting and not giving up. But don't make this choice to get back up by yourself. This is where a personal relationship with God is so important. He commands us not to go at it alone. He gives you and I the courage to not be afraid, and the mental toughness to not get discouraged even when we fall again. I'm so glad my daughter chose to get back up after her numerous falls off of the beam. It gave her the fortitude she would need for her future falls. Your knock downs will test your grit too. Like Daniel did in the movie, *The Karate Kid*, keep your eye on your coach (God), He will give you the stamina to get back up. And after a few knock downs, your determination to get back up will land you a spot on the champion podium. You're standing stronger, with valor and victory, because you chose to get back on your feet, and not stay on the ground.

Getting back up is *Better Than Espresso*

Reflecting on Life's Knock Downs

❖ In what way(s) do you feel life is repeatedly knocking you down?

❖ Why do you think it's difficult for you to get back up?

❖ The Karate Kid kept his eye on his coach who gave him courage to get back up. We can't get back up by ourselves either. I invite you to consider God as your coach. Spend a minute inviting God in to be your coach. (Here's a simple prayer you can recite).

God, I need the courageYou gave Joshua. I have been knocked down so many times and I don't know how to get up anymore. I admit, I can't get up by myself. I need Your help. Help me to fix my eyes on you and not my circumstances. Reveal to me that You are my "refuge and strength." Help me to get off the floor right now and infuse in me Your strength and courage. Amen

Day 6

Comparison is a Trap, it Can Kill My Confidence

Each one should test their own actions. Then they can take pride in themselves alone, without comparing themselves to someone else, for each one should carry their own load.
(Galatians 6:4-5)

A glimpse of heaven! Land of big palm trees and white sandy beaches is the picturesque view of the Florida Keys. It was certainly a family vacation we will never forget.

I was fascinated at how many iguanas live in South Florida. On our first day, we journeyed to the pool. I was ready to bask in the Florida sun, relax, read my books, and work on my golden graham tan. Not ten minutes into my tanning, my kids scurried over to our lounge chairs excited to share all the iguanas they just scouted. Suddenly, a huge, thorny, green iguana passed by my lounge chair. We then realized we were *surrounded* by these friendly creatures, hiding in the lush green bushes.

I grabbed my camera, not wanting to miss out on this perfect picture moment. As I walked around the pool area with my son, we looked intently into the bushes and saw more iguanas, camouflaged on bright green tree branches. They looked so peaceful, and relaxed, just taking it easy. As we looked closer, I realized the beauty of these creatures. From a distance, they all appeared the same, blending in with their natural habitat. But, as we gazed closer, they were each quite different. Each one had its unique spots, texture, and colors.

Iguanas use their camouflage trait to blend in with their environment. That is their defense mechanism against their predators. They are afraid to stand out, as this poses a threat to their safety.

I can be just like an iguana. It's easier and safer to *blend in*. Blending in though often causes me to compare myself to those around me. I want the gifts, talents, and abilities other women have. I don't want to be different because what I have doesn't seem to be as valuable as what they have. I am too afraid to showcase my true colors – afraid my colors aren't as beautiful when compared to other women.

Can you relate? Do you ever feel like you are stuck in comparison mode, not knowing how to become free? Often, I feel like I am alone, trapped by my need to compare myself to others, yet not realizing I am imprisoned by this feeling.

Comparison Relates to Confidence

The problem with comparison is it eventually kills our confidence at some point or another. It blinds us to our own beautiful and colorful spots like the iguanas, keeping us stuck and not living up to our fullest potential. When comparison dominates me, it's because I am lacking confidence. Naturally, I place more pressure to look good, be accepted by others, and yearn for the "likes", "emojis", and the "hands of applause". A lesson I continue to learn as I am "adulting" (lingo from my college-age daughter) is when I'm stuck in comparison, it tells me I am not satisfied or at ease with my God-given colorful spots. Proverbs 14:14 (NKJV) says, "The backslider in heart will be filled with his own ways, but a good man will be satisfied from above." I don't want to be filled with a superficial image, I want to empty that image. I want to focus on accepting and embracing my authentic, colorful spots, and not be consumed by the temptation to compare them. This really is the secret to living a satisfied life. Depression is rampant in our world today and studies are linking this epidemic to the negative effects of social media comparison and the need for "likes" and applause.

Lack of confidence is one reason we get stuck in comparison. I think the areas we compare most are the areas we feel less than or the areas we feel empty (looks, intelligence, friendliness, personality, marriages, homes, careers, etc.). Sure, we all have some sort of damaging background or struggle we are trying to fight, but confidence is a learned art and a faith factor. As Galatians 6:4 instructs, test your own actions (Why are you comparing? Is there a void that is causing you to compare?) so you can respond to your own calling with a sense of honoring pride. If you lack confidence, it's not too late to ask God for more of it. Remember, He is the One who created your colorful spots so examine your soul and ask God to reveal those unique spots. Once your God-confidence (not puffed-up self) begins to rumble, comparison begins to crumble. When this happens, celebrate – because your life will be more noticed, God-honoring, and admirable. You will have more capacity to sit with a woman and hear the struggle in her story, instead of judging your impressions of her outer story. That is what we are all called to do – *make a difference* in someone's life, not compare and contrast them with *our* lives.

> *Once your God-confidence (not puffed-up self) begins to rumble, comparison begins to crumble.*

Is comparison killing your God-given confidence? If so, can you contemplate the iguana illustration and take a step back, and acknowledge and affirm the colorful spots that make you special, unique, and different? Celebrate your natural bent instead of "blending in" with your neighbor's natural bent. Celebrate your friend's colorful spots too. This is how you and I will beat comparison. Then, ask God how you can use your natural bent – your unique colorful spots – to influence the world around you. No doubt, He will show you!

Celebrating instead of comparing is *Better Than Espresso*

Reflecting on Your Uniqueness

❖ Imagine a sense of peace from not feeling you have to compare yourself every time you scroll through your friends' timelines on social media. Here's an honest question: Do you feel better about yourself or worse after spending 30 minutes catching up on social media?

❖ Write your thoughts in the space below. (consider if there is a void in your life that is causing you to compare).

❖ Examine who you are as a person. List in the space below the special traits, talents, and strengths you know are inside of you that make you unique:
- My unique traits:

- My natural talents:

- My character and behavioral strengths:

- How can you celebrate the special qualities you listed above? Ask God to show you how you can use your natural bents (your unique spots) to make a difference in this world. Write down any thoughts that come to your mind about how God might be speaking to your heart right now.

Day 7

Losing Makes Me Better

"Very truly I tell you, unless a kernel of wheat falls to the ground and dies, it remains only a single seed. But if it dies, it produces many seeds."
(John 12:24)

I am so tired of losing. When is my life going to start winning?

If you have a competitive spirit like me, you understand the pain of losing. I started taking tennis lessons a few years ago and I've discovered the game constantly tests my ability to lose. I usually play with a gal who is more skilled than me. She challenges my game and creates an opportunity for me to run all over the court! She beats me nearly *every time.* I can recall winning only one or two games. Worse yet,

I sometimes play with my husband, who has never taken lessons a day in his life, and *he* beats me almost every time. Ugh! This really is a frustrating sport. You'd think after walking away a loser so many times, I would quit.

I believe it's in our human nature to defy losing. Too many losses and not enough wins can surely break *anyone's* confidence and ability to persevere. It's tough to gain the courage and perseverance needed to march forward after numerous defeats. This emotion is familiar not only in my game of tennis, but in life. Loss of a friendship, loss of a job, loss of a dream, have all taken a toll on my courage, confidence and emotional health.

As horrible and intense as it is, losing molds us into something better if we persevere. How many times do we see Olympic athletes, professional teams, businesses, or dying marriages come back to life after a season of loss? Michael Jordan, noted as one the best NBA players of all time, said: "I've lost almost 300 games. Twenty-six times I've been trusted to take the game-winning shot... and missed. I've failed over and over in my life. And that is why I succeed". [1] For Michael Jordan, losing helped him learn to get better and ultimately succeed at his game. *Learn* is the key word when it comes to losing. It is impossible to gain a win if we are not willing to learn from losing. I pay my tennis coach because I want to get better at the sport. His job is to point out my mistakes and weaknesses, but it's my job to learn from them. Otherwise, my money goes to waste.

Loss Produces New Growth

At a pivotal point in His ministry, when Jesus was nearing His death, He said this to try to help His followers understand why it was necessary for Him to die:

"Very truly I tell you, unless a kernel of wheat falls to the ground and dies, it remains only a single seed. But if it dies, it produces many seeds" (John 12:24).

A kernel of wheat is a life-bearing seed and can produce a multitude of wheat. However, it must first fall to the ground, be buried, and die underground. It's the process of death that produces nourishment for the seed to reproduce. Jesus represents the kernel of wheat. God had to become man (through Jesus) so death could enter the picture. God provided the death of man as a means of producing new life in our soul. The fruit that resulted from Jesus' death is the outpouring of His love and grace bestowed on our lives. Because of His death, you and I can experience the gift of forgiveness. The unkind words we speak to our spouses or children when they frustrate us, no longer need to guilt and shame us. Death erases the guilt; it renews us, teaches us, and allows us to learn better next time.

If your life feels like a multitude of defeats, perhaps God is trying to cause something to die so that it later produces more fruit than you can imagine. You may be in the middle of what looks like a losing marriage or you may have just been laid off from your job. These are difficult moments indeed, and the loss is too much to bear in the moment. This chapter is probably hard to read because you're asking yourself, *How can this loss help me get better if I have no more strength to proceed?* You can't answer that question right now, but I promise there will be a day when the answer will make sense. It's difficult to comprehend this imagery when you are in the thick of losing. Right now, keep this thought in the back of your head, *your losses may be going through a time of burial.* Like the kernel of wheat, as it remains underground, the required nourishment causes it to reproduce – not just a little increase, but a *surge* of increase. Can you envision how this process will impact you someday? Because of your will to hold on and learn from your loss, your re-growth may look like a renewed person with a better, kinder spirit. Something in your life may need to die so a precious relationship can be rekindled. Your prior job perhaps didn't provide the sharper skills you needed to learn, but your future job will teach you skills you never imagined. Our losses resemble seeds. Sometimes they need to die so our soil becomes more fertile, and the deadened branches bear riper fruit. What a glorious day that will be to see how our losses turn into successes. I'm anticipating the day when all my tennis defeats will begin to result in more triumphs.

As God produces new growth from our seeds of loss, we become better. Our fruit is depositing God's genuine love and grace upon ourselves and others. We spend less time beating ourselves up and more time lifting others off the

> *When we can help others be better, we enhance our own endeavors.*

ground from their fall. When we can help others be better, we enhance our own endeavors.

Our losses fall and die, but it's our perseverance that makes them grow and develop.

Perseverance is *Better Than Espresso*

Reflecting on Losing

❖ Considering the analogy of the kernel of wheat, is there something you currently need to let die so it can regrow and reproduce? (A dream, a friendship, an attitude, a habit?)

❖ Why do you think God may be calling it to die?

❖ You may not feel strong right now, but think about past lessons you learned in your season of losses. Identify that loss. How did God transform you and make you better? Write that thought down in the space below and cement it in your mind as you go through loss either now, or in the future.

– My situation of loss:

– God helped me be better by:

Day 8

My Confidence
Grows Stronger as
God Delivers

David said to Saul, "Let no one lose heart on
account of this Philistine; your servant will go
and fight him."
(1 Samuel 17:32)

D o you have a passion, but through a series of struggles, you've lost your confidence?

My oldest daughter's passion is soccer, which ex-
plodes when she's on the field. Her dream to play at the college level came true.

This was not an easy achievement for her, to say the least.
While in high school, she encountered multiple injuries and
endured two ACL surgeries. She weathered the storm and
continued to do all she could to prepare for her college dream.
Her first year of college was painful, sitting on the sidelines

and not being able to play in the game due to her injury. She knew she had a big hill to climb her second year to earn a starter position. The Big Announcement finally came. Which girls made the travel team for their first away games at two big Universities. My girl was so excited, hoping and praying she would be chosen for the travel team, as she was ready, having worked laboriously for it.

She *didn't* make the travel team.

Brianna's confidence was completely shattered, and disappointment set in once again. As I cried with my daughter over the phone, I tried to console her. She couldn't reason why she was not chosen. From her perspective, she was more passionate about the sport than other girls who made the travel team. Self-doubt raged through her mind in thoughts that said, *I'm not good enough; I am a failure.* I knew those painful emotions too well and how they can strip confidence. I didn't want my daughter to mirror my struggles where I lacked confidence. I wanted to hide my own struggles and protect her from my insecurity. But, I knew this was an opportunity to be an example and help her see the bigger picture behind her emotions. Her confidence was attached to her performance like mine. I knew first-hand the damage that is done if our confidence is solely rooted in ourselves. Her situation was an excellent opportunity to speak truth into my daughter's soul. I reminded her that God uses our upsets to draw us closer to Him. Our confidence grows stronger in the moments we bring God into the equation. Our disappointments provide the means to watch how God delivers.

As moms, we can coach our daughters to be great successes by our own transparent thoughts and sentiments. By sharing our own struggles, we can help them not repeat our unhealthy emotions, habits, and reactions to disappointments.

Have you had a similar experience in which your confidence was shattered because you weren't chosen, didn't attain a level of success you expected, or worst yet, got intimidated by the words of a bully?

A New Confidence

Just as our confidence can be easily shattered, it can also grow stronger when we see God as our deliverer. A break in our spirit is not the end of our story. You may consider yourself a person who lacks assurance. But if you give the master builder a chance, God uses His hammer and nails to rebuild your confidence, even re-developing it into something greater. Perhaps you have formed a damaging habit of placing limits on your abilities, because someone told you in the past, "you're not smart enough to do that." But there's a greater builder inside of you who can reconstruct that bullied thought and give you the hope of poise and tenacity. *How would your life look differently if you soared with this new level of confidence?* You would probably be accomplishing things you never imagined.

The story of David and Goliath is an all-time favorite (even if you didn't grow up in Sunday School). David was a young shepherd boy, small in stature and definitely not a valiant warrior to fight the giant, Goliath. Goliath was trying to destroy God's people. David's confidence to fight this terrifying giant did not develop as a result of his outer physique or warrior training or talent. His confidence was completely centered on trust in his almighty God. You see, God delivered David earlier in his shepherding years from both a lion and a bear. Based on God's track record of rescuing him in the past, David was confident that God could deliver him *again* from the hand of an even bigger enemy. *David's confidence got stronger because he trusted and saw how God delivered.*

David spoke bold words to the 9-foot giant in front of him: "You come against me with sword and spear and javelin, but I come against you in the name of the Lord Almighty, the God of the armies of Israel, whom you have defied" (1 Samuel 17:45). Wow, what courage. And what powerful words.

David fought his enemy with the confidence of *God's* character as opposed to relying on his own merit.

I was proud of my daughter. After time had settled, she was able to gain perspective and put the emotion behind her. She didn't allow this adversity to ruin her mindset, but instead, she remained positive, and continued to show up even when it was hard on her ego. Remaining steadfast and a commitment to trust in her ability, helped her not to waver. Confidence grows because we choose to show up, not give up, and attempt the difficult and uncomfortable. Confidence depletes when we stay stagnate, don't take chances, and ditch the difficult. It's like a muscle, confidence is strengthened the more it is exercised. God had delivered my daughter with her past upsets and challenges, and He would deliver her again. Like David, as we witness God's deliverance in our past, our future is designed with more determination.

> *Confidence grows because we choose to show up, not give up.*

How do *you* grab hold of more confidence during your moments of struggle and disappointment? Does your confidence stream from your own merit, or knowing full well the almighty works of God in your life? Is there a moment you can recall when God rescued you from a struggle and built back your morale? Those should be the reminders of why you and I can be more confident. They assure us that we'll have success with God and that our victories will be a result of His deliverance from our moment of insecurity and self-doubt.

A new confidence is *Better Than Espresso*

Reflecting on Your Confidence

❖ On a scale from 1-10, how would you rate your confidence at this moment? (1 as no confidence, 10 as highly confident): _____

❖ What has contributed to your confidence or lack of it?

❖ Confidence grows if we are willing to show up, not give up. Are you showing up or giving up? (answer this honestly so God can hear your heart)

❖ When we show up, despite the lack of courage, that's when God delivers, and your confidence grows stronger. If you answered "no" in the above question, let God hear your heart right now. Write down where you need to show up, and then write a prayer to God. I'm excited to see how God will deliver His confidence to you ☺

  - I need to show up by:

  - My prayer to God:

Day 9

Just Start and Don't Worry About Being Great

"Your beginnings will seem humble, so prosperous will your future be."
(Job 8:7)

What did you start, but quit because you didn't see yourself as great?

Starting something new can be intimidating. A diet, going back to school, a business idea, a relationship? Why is it difficult for most of us to start something? Sometimes it's because we just don't know how to start, but other times I believe our shame of failure prevents us from starting. Humble beginnings are tough. Our perfectionistic brains tell us we can't start until we are *great*. What a lie!

If we are not starting because we don't know how, that is no excuse. Today it's easier than it's ever been to get whatever directions we need within moments, information is at our fingertips – and on our computers, tablets and phones – immediately! Talk to someone with experience, learn all you can about the very thing you want to start. Information, wisdom, encouragement is the fuel that will move you in the right direction. One of the greatest pieces of advice I heard recently is if you want to start living a dream inside your heart, place yourself in proximity to a person who is already achieving it. That may look like setting up a coffee date with someone and asking them how they got to where they are. Or, maybe it means pursuing an internship and learning a new skill.

If you are like me, you struggle with a bit of perfectionism. You have this grand illusion that if you are not great at something from the beginning, you will fall short and then you will regret starting. I have fed my mind that lie for most of my life. For a long time, I had the desire to speak to women and write a book, but I never considered myself a writer and my speaking skills needed improvement. I don't know why I have this ideal that I need to be a big leaguer at the beginning. I guess I'm scared to flounder and as I get older, my fear of failure heightens. I also have this bad habit of looking at experienced writers and speakers and shaming myself against their work. *I'll never be as good as that person, and if I can't be talented like her, then it's no use.* Look how damaging that mindset is. Do you, too, struggle with beginning something like I did? Finally, I was tired of sabotaging myself, so I decided to start. I made a coffee date with someone I knew who was living my dream. Looking back now, all I needed was the encouragement and extra push to pursue the potential I had but never gave myself credit for. With social media at our fingertips, we tend to see what we perceive as "the great" and think, *I am not that great so why bother?* Girlfriend, this is the biggest lie the enemy is feeding our culture today. *Don't give in to it.* I admit, it is humbling to begin something new, especially if we aren't sure we have what it takes. But this is where our faith is practiced.

Our Start is Humbling

Job 8:7 warns us that our beginnings will humble us, but look at the promise at the end. Our futures will be prosperous. This is encouraging to me. How about you? For a writer, humble beginnings are being rejected over and over by publishers. As a speaker, it's walking off the platform not sure if the audience connected with my message. These have been my humble beginnings and many times I have just wanted to quit because my lack of greatness scared me. I am persevering though because I know God's intention is to show me grace and comfort. I also know that it's the discipline of starting that's going to lead to progress. I'm sure you want progress too, so can we do this together? *Let's start today and not worry about being great!*

If there is a calling on your life, a passion and desire God has put inside your heart, start going for it. I believe a lot of women are depressed today because they want to start living with more purpose, but they don't do what is required to start. Fear has paralyzed them, so they stay stuck in the mud with this passion and desire and go nowhere. Don't be one of them. Rise above it by taking that first step to start. I can write this, because I was one of them. You, my friend, just need to start like I did. This book would have never happened if I didn't put myself out there and put my fingers to the keyboard – *even while I lacked courage.* Your first step will give you the dose of confidence you need for your next step. You will be amazed at your progress as one customer turns into multiple customers. A year later, you will look back astonished by your first steps and thankful you persevered and didn't give into the lie that said, *I have to be great.* Most importantly, take this desire, dream, and passion to God in prayer. Ask God to give you the courage to start and not worry about being great. As you begin, keep this thought in the back of your mind:

It's my humble beginnings that will lead to higher places.
That's *Better Than Espresso*

Reflecting on My Start

❖ Look around your house right now. Is there a project you have been delaying, or a task you've been putting off, such as paying a bill, cleaning out cupboards, or following up with some paperwork? Write down what it is you need to start doing in your house right now and then write one plan of action you can do today that will move the process along. (Go ahead, do it now, and then come back to the next question. ☺)

❖ Now, take this same inertia and write down a dream or passion you want to start working toward, but you haven't because you're afraid you aren't great.

- My dream or passion:

❖ What is one action step you can take today or in the next week that will create the movement you need to *start*? If you can't take advantage of the action step this week, give yourself a deadline to take this action step.

   – My first step is:

   – My deadline (date I will take the first step):

You are doing great! Your first step will lead to another step. You are on your way toward God's greatness.

Part 3

When the Burden of Hurt, Pain, and Shame Bind You

Day 10

Heal From Rejection
or it will Become an
Infection

*"You intended to harm me, but God intended it
for good to accomplish what is now being done,
the saving of many lives. So then, don't be
afraid. I will provide for you and your children.
And he reassured them and spoke kindly to
them."*
(Genesis 50: 20-21)

He didn't return my call, he's dumping me."
    "I worked so hard to get that promotion, but someone else received it."

"I didn't get invited to that party, but everyone else did."

How often have you, like me, tried to understand why you weren't chosen? I remember meeting a cute guy at summer camp. You know that guy, the one whom all the girls adore and are fighting over to get his attention. This was that guy. There were more beautiful girls with more dynamic personalities than mine, but I was the one he chose to take on a special date. I felt like a princess. After our date, I fell for him, hard. I was certain he was marriage material. We had such a good time, I was confident he would call me again. A week passed by with no call and I couldn't resist – I called him. There was no answer, just a recording, so I left a cheerful message. I waited excitedly for him to return my call, but my dream was shattered. Obviously, he was not interested in a second date with me. My heart hurt and pounded with rejection.

During my career days, I was an over achiever. I worked hard to impress my bosses and was eager for promotions. I earned my way up to an Assistant Marketing Manager and learned all I could from my Account Manager. She secretly shared that she was leaving the company, so that was my opportunity for a deserved promotion. I interviewed, feeling confident I would be rewarded with the position. Sadly, I was turned down for the promotion. Do you know what it feels like to be confident of success and then blindsided with a no? I was humiliated in front of my peers. What was wrong with me and my work performance? Didn't I deserve that promotion? Another moment (and more would come) of feeling unwanted, unchosen, and dismissed.

Rejection hurts, stings our egos, and is difficult to recover from. You and I are going to experience exclusion at some time or another in our lives. It's inevitable in the fallen world we live in. However, there is a brighter side to our rejection. I know how much it can pierce through our hearts and tear it to shreds in the moment. But, I have found as I work through my rejection, I start to develop tougher skin, which is more beneficial in the long run. The next time I feel set aside, it doesn't take as long to recover. Rejection can be like a bee sting. It hurts in the moment, but we must learn to remove the stinger and let it heal. Otherwise, our initial sting can produce a more serious infection later. I didn't realize how my earlier rejections created residue in my heart. As life progressed, the uninvited emotions became more difficult to process. I didn't equip my mind to heal from the wounds of my past, therefore serious infections developed later.

Reframe Rejection

I'm learning to handle rejection better by reframing my "no's," instead of wallowing in them. Most likely, God has a teachable moment for us in the "no," such as developing our character, faith, and perseverance. Perhaps our "no" is meant to steer us toward another path that better suits our personalities and temperaments. I know this language all sounds well and good. The reality is, when we are in the thick of it, we don't care about the lesson because it hurts our tender hearts too much.

The story of Joseph in Genesis 37-42 epitomizes the raw emotions of rejection. He was a man of high character and integrity, very well liked, especially by his father. He was the youngest son and his brothers were filled with intense jealousy toward Joseph, especially after a dream he decided to share with his brothers. His dream made it appear that Joseph was bragging (and I don't blame his brothers for their jealousy). However, they took it too far and first decided to kill Joseph, but guilt set in and they decided to sell him into slavery instead. Joseph's life took a big U-turn, as suddenly he was living in Egypt, a foreign land, with no family and friends. God was with Joseph though, gave him favor with the Pharaoh, and he prospered in everything he did, including dodging a serious temptation by the wife of a powerful man who employed him.

Rejection from the outside world is difficult enough, but to be repudiated by your own family is a heavy and hurtful emotion to bear. Joseph is a great example of reframing the tough emotion of rejection. Even though he did everything right and was still thrown into prison because of false accusations against him, he remained steadfast. He didn't cave in to his enemies who were trying to destroy him. He remained optimistic, flexible, perseverant, and faithful even in his suffering. Eventually, his ability to reframe paid off and brought blessings not curses to him and his family. He won the favor of Egypt's Pharaoh by interpreting Pharaoh's dreams of a coming famine. Joseph became the hero in the story. Because of his position with the Pharaoh, he had the ability to provide his family with food during a time of severe famine. God used a hurtful moment of rejection in Joseph's life for a greater plan not only for him, but his entire race. God eventually re-united Joseph with his deceitful brothers in order to literally save their lives. Joseph didn't seek retribution from his brothers. Instead, he saw the bigger plan in his pain of rejection. He told his brothers, "You intended to harm me, but God intended it for good (Genesis 50:20).

If you are troubled by the feeling of being set aside and dismissed, think about how you can reframe that situation, so it doesn't infect other areas of your life. Take a moment to dig into the depth of your soul and get curious. Discover why a person's behavior or response is angering you. Is there something in your past that is causing the sting to be so painful? If so, I encourage you to reframe that incident in the past as much as possible, so you can have a better perspective on it today. Yes, the situation may have harmed you, but how can you see in it a situation that God intended for good? Seek to learn the greater lessons like Joseph did, so you can remain steadfast the next time you feel set aside, disregarded, excluded...rejected.

Learning to reframe rejection is
Better Than Espresso

Reflecting on the Sting of Rejection

❖ Think about the last time you felt rejection. Does it still feel like a sting to your heart? Fill in the blanks to help you do a soul inventory:
When this happened (name the situation):

I felt unwanted because:

❖ When we can see how God intended our "set asides" and "no's" for His good, that is a step toward healing. How is God accomplishing something good in your life from a past no or set aside?

❖ If you are currently experiencing rejection, use one of these reframing techniques to get you on the right track toward healing:
   – Get curious about the situation. Why is it maddening you?

–   What open door might exist right now?

–   What lesson might God be trying to teach you?

❖ Great job on reframing your no. You're getting tougher and the sting is not as painful.

Day 11

God Doesn't Fail Me, He Goes Before Me

"The Lord is the one who goes ahead of you; He will be with you He will not fail you or forsake you. Do not fear or be dismayed."
(Deuteronomy 31:8 ESV)

It's so comforting to know I have a tender Father who comes alongside me when I'm hurt and in pain.

During one of my many weekends on the soccer field, I witnessed an emotion we all feel at some time or another. As I was approaching the soccer field, I noticed out of the corner of my eye, a young eager girl who was being coached and trained as a referee. The experienced referee was offering her some tips before she stepped onto the field. She seemed ready and confident.

I set up my chair on the sideline, excited to watch my daughter play. Both teams seemed to be a great match. The newbie referee was on my sideline running up and down the field making calls and throwing up her bright yellow flag. Each time she raised her flag, parents from the other team screamed words of disapproval at the young ref's call. The look on her face spelled... S.H.A.M.E. The screaming match didn't subside, and the poor new referee was humiliated in front of a large audience. She couldn't hold it together and the wet tears started pouring down her face. An older gentleman, looking official in his uniform, came to her rescue and helped her assess the rest of the game. He moved ahead of her, gently instructed her, and did not fail or shame her. It was a beautiful picture of God's tender love and concern for us.

Courage is Available

God desires to see us courageous. Trying something new requires guts. As I read the Scriptures, I am encouraged to see how many times it references "courage." It seems God is trying to get a message across to me: trusting Him leads to courage. In today's verse, Moses was about to die and passed the torch to Joshua to lead the Israelites to the Promised Land. He summoned Joshua to be strong and courageous and remember *God would go before him.* He will not fail in his assignment if God is at the lead. God never leaves us hanging, we can depend on His tender lead.

I'm sure the young gal left the field more empowered the next time she had to referee a game. I imagine the gentle touch of the older gentleman taught her compassion and how to learn from the more experienced. He helped her win a victory of bravery instead of walking away self-defeated. You and I have the same opportunity to lean in and learn how God goes before us, giving us tenacity to handle what is out of our comfort zone and out of our control.

If you are training for something – a new season of motherhood, a new job, a new marriage, a new academic course – and find yourself falling behind, imagine the comforting presence of your heavenly Father going before you. Don't resist His instruction or be frightened or dismayed at His presence. He is not your enemy or an opposing team member. Accept His wise guidance because He is available to coach you, not fail you!

God's coaching skills are *Better Than Espresso*

Reflecting on the One Who Goes Before You

❖ Have you had a coach in your life who has gone before you, encouraging correcting, and cheering you on? _____ If so, who is that person and how has he or she made a difference in your life?

❖ Where do you need God's coaching skills to go before you right now?

❖ Isaiah 30:21 says: Whether you turn to the right or to the left, your ears will hear a voice behind you, saying, "This is the way; walk in it."
What is *your* vision of God? Do you believe He is at your side with a tender heart (like the gentleman in the story), not failing or forsaking you, but loving you and coaching you on? Journal your thoughts below.

Day 12

I'm Learning to Laugh at Myself, Not Shame Myself

A cheerful heart is good medicine,
but a crushed spirit dries up the bones.
(Proverbs 17:22)

I have a story that will be remembered by my family as one of our funniest moments. My parents have an annual tradition with their circle of friends to plan a New Year's getaway. One year they planned their getaway at the Hotel del Coronado in San Diego. It is quite a classy hotel full of sophisticated people, not your typical Best Western Motel for traveling tourists. My parents checked in at the front desk and proceeded to their room. Dad was amazed and excited at all the goodies stashed in a beautiful basket on the counter top and drinks in the refrigerator. They thought to themselves, "how nice for a hotel to provide *free* snacks and drinks for their guests." As the weekend went on, they didn't resist. In fact, they *indulged* and enjoyed every kind of snack.

On the last day, when it was time to check out, they didn't want to waste the uneaten snacks. So, Mom decided to stash her overnight bag with all the unopened snacks. As they prepared to pay their bill at the front desk, a perplexed look swept over their faces. They noticed all the charges for snacks they fully enjoyed during their stay. The attendant informed them that there is a charge for the room snacks. With sheer shock and embarrassment, they mentioned to the attendant they were unaware of this policy and proceeded to unload their overnight bag at the front counter with all the unopened snacks. Friends and patrons were watching the entire event. Can't you just feel the sense of embarrassment? Talk about being on center stage with complete vulnerability!

What I admire about my parents, is they didn't hibernate from their shame and embarrassment. They laughed out loud with all their friends. Laughter minimizes our shame.

Another memory related to laughter in the vulnerable moments, is when my daughter and I attended the U.S. Gymnastic Olympic Trials. Half-time entertainment was a young Disney TV star Laura Marano, from *Austin & Ally*, performing one of her first live concerts. Five minutes into her performance, her bright red lipstick moved from her lips to her entire lower jaw. Clearly her microphone was too close for comfort! She was totally unaware that her lower face was covered in bright red lipstick and the entire audience could see this debacle magnified on the big arena screens. The tech team apparently came to her rescue and when she ended her song, instead of

> **Laughter minimizes our shame.**

running off stage humiliated, she turned to her fans and made a funny joke. What an example for our young girls to see a TV star handle her vulnerable moment with laughter instead of shame.

Laughter is Good for the soul

Laughter in the vulnerable moments keeps shame at a distance. It's not easy feeling exposed and embarrassed. Most **people** want to appear that they have it all together, so laughter in the embarrassing moments is difficult. But the truth is, if we can laugh at ourselves, it minimizes our shame and produces a spirit of cheer rather than a crushed spirit. It minimizes the laborious effort of protecting our perfect reputations. Learning to laugh out loud at our stupid mistakes can serve us quite well. Laughter heals our wounds of striving to be perfect, so we appear to have it all together.

I enjoy being around people who can laugh. Wouldn't you agree that people who can turn an embarrassing incident into something to laugh about are usually happier with themselves? They are not stuck in the shame of trying to portray a perfect image to the world. They are refreshing to be around, good medicine for the soul. A study by the University of Maryland concluded that laughter and a sense of humor can protect against heart disease (Science Daily, 2000). Hence, a crushed, shamed, and too serious spirit, can be the thief that steals your joy and robs your life.

Even in our most vulnerable, shameful, and crushed spirit moments, there is room to be cheerful. But you probably agree it's difficult to possess this spirit of cheer on your own. God wants to extend His mercy as much as possible when we go through times of suffering and even embarrassment. He loves us that much. I think God places us in situations and with people during those times when He knows it's laughter that will lift our heavy hearts. As I think about the story above with Ally performing with lipstick all over her face, maybe there was someone in the audience that needed a good laugh to alleviate their crushed spirit. Maybe your embarrassing moment was meant to bring laughter to a crushed spirit around you. The next time you are shamed by an embarrassing moment, can you see it differently? Perhaps you were supposed to shatter the crowd's image of perfection and help them relax and be at ease in their own shameful and embarrassing moments.

Can you turn your awkward moment into a laughable event? Share it with a trusted friend and practice the joy of laughing instead of holding onto the shame. Exercising this habit allows you to learn the important lesson of loving your imperfections and prevents a crushed spirit.

Laughter is *Better Than Espresso*

Reflecting on Your Ability to Laugh

❖ Is there an incident you can recall that imparted shame or embarrassment? Write out that incident below and how it made you feel.

❖ Can you laugh about that humbling moment now? Why or why not?

❖ If this is a season in which your spirit is crushed, take some time right now and focus your mind on something cheerful and good from your past. Write it down in the space below as a visual and reminder that "cheerful moments" are ahead again. Pray for God to remind of you of His promise, "suffering is only for a little while and soon He will restore your strength" (1 Peter 5:10).

❖ Here's a fun exercise. Search the term "Funniest Videos Ever" on your computer, tablet or smartphone. Get with a friend, spouse, or family member and let yourself laugh out loud (like my junior higher is doing right now as she is watching her YouTube funny videos). Laughter is such a refreshing sound.

Day 13

Staying in My Past
Paralyzes My Present

See, I am doing a new thing!
Now it springs up; do you not perceive it?
I am making a way in the wilderness
and streams in the wasteland."
(Isaiah 43:19)

As you stare into your past, how does it make you feel? Does your past bring great joy, sadness, or anger? Has it been filled with tragedy and disappointment which has caused you to stay stagnate and afraid? Or do you acknowledge the detriments of your past, but choose to see joy in new lessons learned?

I admit, I have allowed some of the pain of my past to paralyze my present and my future. I want to move forward, but all I see ahead is the bright orange "danger" sign blaring in the headlights, causing me to retreat. My new path looks rocky, slippery, "dangerous" and I don't want to embark on this risk again, it's too scary. It's just easier to justify staying in "my comfy little place" so I don't feel the pain all over again.

Are you cuddled up with your fleece blanket, too, staying in the easy and comfortable? Have you created a mental picture in your mind of your past and it's causing a fear to dwell inside you? You're hanging out too much with Mr. Comfortable and Mrs. Stagnate who are your worst enemies. They don't want you to move forward in your purpose and in healthy relationships because that requires getting out of the comfort zone. These travel companions are not helping you explore an exciting future. They are reminding you of the harsh words spoken to you by a parent, sibling, or teacher who said, "you don't have what it takes to be ...." Or maybe it was that bullyish girl who made you feel so worthless with her cruel words. Our companions remind us how familiar and easier it is to stay in our painful pasts. I can certainly understand why we get stuck in our past, justify it, and have a difficult time moving forward.

Our Past is Training Ground for the Future

Life is meant to be a journey. I am not sure why we have this idea that we must *arrive*. I guess it's the pressure from the world we live in. Our imperfect world defines our past as messy and traumatic, and it's natural to camp out in those places. But the beautiful promise of God is that He is all about doing *new things* in your life. Your past is training ground for what God wants to do with your future. Let's fix our eyes and thoughts on Isaiah 43:19 (at the beginning of this chapter) for a minute.

God was reminding His people (the Israelites) of how He took care of them hundreds of years earlier by helping them escape slavery in Egypt. God was reminding them to trust again, He was bringing them back to their homeland, Israel. At that time in history, the Israelites were enslaved again by the Babylonians. God promised to care for them once again, but with a different purpose and new lessons. Don't forget God's mercies of your past, but always be mindful how He may be springing up a new lesson for your new season. God desires you to perceive the *new thing* He is accomplishing. Why is it so easy to "push the rewind button" on the events of our past? Probably because it's familiar to us. For me, I have recognized how damaging and disabling my rewind button keeps me from moving into new and exciting territory. There are valuable lessons to learn by pushing rewind, but pushing the forward button should be more of a habit. I know there is a fresh water oasis ahead of me, but to enjoy it, my past needs to be in the past. Do you push rewind more than you should? I'm sure you too would like to experience more oasis than wasteland. So, let's together agree to only push rewind for learning sake and not camp there, but let it groom us for our forward future.

God is preparing an oasis for you, don't allow your wasteland to dry you up. See your wasteland as preparation for the new; a restored relationship with a friend or loved one. He may be trying to heal your hurts and pains that have sabotaged your future. I encourage you to find the life-giving water in this difficult wasteland. It will quench your broken heart and advance you into new and increased territory. Instead of ignoring the *new thing* God has for you, perceive it, own it, and notice the mouth-watering streams that are present even in your wasteland moments.

Your "New Thing" is *Better Than Espresso*

Reflecting on a New Thing

❖ If you are like me, you enjoy buying a new outfit for a special event. Something new evokes a special emotion and feeling inside. What has been your *something new* lately? (A newly decorated house, a new child, a new car, a new job or position? A new relationship?)

❖ What emotion has your *something new* evoked in you?

❖ Our lives contain seasons in which we are in an oasis or a wasteland. An oasis is the fertile area where water and growth is found. A wasteland is the desert – a dry and absent place.
What *new things* has God shown you in both your oasis and wasteland moments? List them below in the chart:
Oasis_____ Wasteland

Day 14

My Hard Moments
Humble Me,
Not Harm Me

Humble yourselves before the Lord, and He will lift you up.
(James 4:10)

The reigning gymnastics champion took an unexpected fall on all four events. Sheer shock covered the spectators' faces.

My youngest daughter is a competing gymnast. The last meet of the season was a difficult moment for one of the girls on her team. She had always been the expected champion, but not this time. This little girl is a go-getter, perfectionist, hard on herself, and definitely not used to losing. She was crushed by her performance, not winning a single medal. I guess you could say, she tasted a bit of humility that particular day. I remember my daughter learning a similar lesson early on in her career. She, too, always scored in the top four places but at one of her last meets, she didn't come home with a single medal. Ouch, that was a punch to her ego.

We have all heard the saying, "It keeps us humble." A dose of humility is good for all our souls, but it doesn't discount the hurt and pain it can create. In my humble moments, especially where it reflects my performance, (like the gymnast), I can feel shame. Sometimes even embarrassed. Humility can be embarrassing and even shameful, but in the long run, it does more good than harm.

The Promise in the Humble

There is encouragement for you and me as we endure the meek, difficult moments. God's promise is that when we humble ourselves, He lifts us up. Humbling ourselves before God does not have to be a public event. It takes place in the privacy of your heart and your prayer closet. It's a time to admit to God the area in your heart that may have demonstrated a selfish-ness, a prideful ambition, or an impure motive in your moment of loss. Like athletes, our losses may be for the purpose of learning humility. Do you notice how the proud and cocky athlete who gets humbled by his flawed performance, seems to have a sweeter, softer spirit later? Spectators then seem to enjoy them more. Not many people respect the cocky, but they honor the humble. It's the same with God. First Peter 5:5 says *He resists the proud.* He knows the potential damage done if our hearts becomes too prideful. He warns us that our pride goes before a fall (Proverbs 16:18). His usual response is to tweak whatever selfish ambition led to our pride. That may look like going through a disappointing loss. Not an easy endeavor, but the silver lining is *He always lifts up the humble.* Pride is not an easy subject to talk about, but it's a natural enemy and we *all* need to fight against it at one time or another.

As you and I resist a heart of pride, something beautiful begins to happen. God takes our petty pride and replaces it with our better side. Former judgmental thoughts then become positive, prayerful thoughts. That friend's marriage we used to talk about and criticize is now bathed with understanding and prayer. We are given eyes of compassion instead of judgment for that friend's

> **God takes our petty pride and replaces it with our better side.**

child whom we didn't necessarily like. We develop a new and pleasant side to our individual personalities as we resist pride and embrace humility. The most apparent change is we understand God's grace in a whole new way. Perhaps you may have experienced it for the first time. He lifts you from the pit of despair. He lifts your reputation to a new level. He gives you more love from your spouse and kids. He begins to promote you, instead of demote you. He pours favor over your ambitions because you give Him the glory and don't steal it for yourself. You begin winning again, because you have learned how to be humbled by the hard situations.

As we learn the lesson of humility, the next time we are knocked down we will be reminded of how He lifted us up. A year later, I witnessed the "softer side" of the gymnast who was humbled by her performance. She was more relaxed in her style and gave herself more grace when she messed up. She became friendlier with other top gymnasts. Her ambition seemed tempered, not centered around herself. It really is amazing how we change when we are humbled. God is not out to get you or refuse you when the difficult moments of loss strike. His desire is to lift you up and adorn you with His mercy and grace.

God's lifting is *Better Than Espresso*

Reflecting on Your Humble Moments

❖ What thoughts, reactions, and feelings come to mind when you hear the word *humble* or *humility?*

❖ Why do you think you respond or react that way?

❖ Have you had an experience like the gymnast in which you "fell hard" and it humbled you? Use the space to reflect on this memory and how it made you feel.

❖ Think about it. How have you ultimately been changed through humility and how has God lifted you up? His promise of lifting you up is so good!

Day 15

My Broken Pieces Prepare Me for a Breakthrough

In her deep anguish Hannah prayed to the Lord, weeping bitterly. And she made a vow, saying, "Lord Almighty, if you will only look on your servant's misery and remember me, and not forget your servant but give her a son, then I will give him to the Lord for all the days of his life, and no razor will ever be used on his head." ...So in the course of time, Hannah became pregnant and gave birth to a son. She named him Samuel, saying, "Because I asked the Lord for him."
(1 Samuel 1: 11, 20)

H ave you ever broken something of value? A piece of your grandma's china, an expensive necklace, your child's cherished toy? Not too long ago, I got into my husband's brand-new car, pulled into reverse, and slowly backed out of the driveway, trying to navigate around another parked car and the cement wall right next to me. I turned my wheel too sharp and heard a dreaded scratching noise. *Ouch!* A big scratch mark with chipped paint now marred his new powder blue sports car. I felt terrible and full of shame that I was not more careful. We are people who don't like things broken, especially when those things are dear to us – or someone else. Breaking something can often make us feel guilty, shameful, and unworthy.

None of us like to feel anything resembling chipped paint on a shiny new car. But sometimes, life just feels broken. If you are like me, I desperately want to fix what feels broken. If you have studied the Enneagram (a personality profile), then you know all about type 3: The Achiever. This was one of my highest scores. A type 3 is driven by achievement and only feels valued by what they achieve. When I don't perform up to my high expectations, my ego can resemble a shattered piece of glass; fragmented and disfigured. I realize this mindset is warped but it's difficult for this personality type to accept. It's the cracked part of the Enneagram 3 personality. We all have cracks in our personality that can break us into a thousand, shattered, mosaic pieces.

I have learned that...

God uses my broken pieces to prepare me for a necessary BREAKTHROUGH!

Hannah was a woman in the Bible who felt like her life resembled a broken piece of china. She was a woman which you may possibly relate to; she was unable to conceive a child and enjoy the pleasures of motherhood. I imagine her struggle of not feeling worthy, valued, and important, was especially tough because in biblical days, childbearing was where a woman found her identity. Her heart's cry and prayers to the

Lord probably became exhausting. But, *in the course of time,* God blessed her with a beautiful son. Not an ordinary son, but an influential son who became one of Israel's greatest prophets and priests and anointed the first two kings of Israel.

Can you relate to Hannah and her need for a breakthrough? Where do you need progress and improvement in your life? Breakthroughs remind me of the rays of the sun trying to break through dark, cloudy skies. Sometimes the breakthrough is a glorious sight, watching the strong, bright rays pierce fiercely through the dark, grey sky. The sun's light brings a sense of joy, comfort, gladness, warmth especially after long, dreary, cloudy days. I'm sure Hannah was elated to see the breakthrough of the sun in her own life. Her longing for a child finally came true. She had a child who would be used by God in greater ways than she imagined. A breakthrough! No longer a life that felt defective. Her story certainly became a light, an example how God provides breakthrough and then brings abundant increase to the area we feel most fragmented.

> **Breakthrough! No longer a life that feels defective.**

Hannah's story is a reminder to both you and me. God hears the cries of our hearts and our surrendered prayers play a critical role for our biggest breakthroughs. Places that feel shattered will one day be on display as a beautiful mosaic. Be encouraged. Your piece of art will be a ray of light for another mosaic that's in the process of being molded back together.

Breakthrough is *Better Than Espresso*

Reflecting on Your Shattered Mosaic

❖ Is there a piece of your life, like Hannah's, where your spirit has been broken? Is it a recent pain or something you have been trying to fix for a long time? Identify it and describe it in the space below.

❖ Two important lessons to remember when life feels broken:
- Prayer and time are absolutely necessary for a breakthrough.
- Opposition often precedes a breakthrough.

What opposition are you facing right now? Consider this opposition as a reminder that God is in your breakthroughs.

❖ When we need breakthrough, the book of Psalms has powerful scriptures. I especially like Psalm 91. (NIV) Take a moment and meditate on these verses. What "sticky truth" can you capture in your mind today from these verses?

- "He is my refuge and my fortress" (vs 2)
- "He will cover you with his feathers, under his wings you will find refuge" (vs4)
- "He will call on me, and I will answer him" (vs 15)
-

❖ If you would like a sticky truth to recite daily, go to my website (juliepearson.org) and order a "mirror decal" to stick on your bathroom mirror to remind you to pray because breakthrough is coming.

Part 4

When You Feel Lost in Your Purpose and Direction

Day 16

Don't Resist My Re-route, *Embrace* it

"Trust in the LORD with all your heart and lean
not on your own understanding; in all your ways
submit to him, and he will make your
paths straight."
(Proverbs 3:5-6)

S iri was bugging me! Isn't her voice annoying sometimes, especially when you are driving?

I'm probably not the only person who has experienced frustration with Siri on my Maps app. It's easy to question her directions to our destinations.

It was a Saturday morning and I was preparing to drive my son to his soccer tournament which was about an hour south of our home. I entered the address into my phone sure of the direction, but as I glanced at my screen, I couldn't believe my eyes – a complete re-route with blue lines everywhere which made absolutely no sense. The Maps app re-routed our journey in the opposite direction. Instead of south, it ordered me to go north. I thought to myself, *Siri has surely lost her mind.* I was not going to follow her directions. She was going to make us late. I ignored her and proceeded with my own directions instead. Annoyed at Siri's voice continually correcting my decision, I decided to tune her out and turn her off. Soon enough, I realized that was a monumental mistake.

It so happened that Siri was right! She really is the master of navigation and as hard as it is to admit, her intuition is better than mine. I should have listened to her all along. I discovered during the drive that there was a big accident, enough to delay our arrival time, which made perfect sense for Siri to re-route us. Instead of embracing the re-route, I resisted it, causing us to arrive a half hour later and my son to fall apart at the seams because he was late for his game. There was a benefit to the re-route, but I foolishly saw it as a curse.

Often, we don't realize there is something bigger behind the scenes when our plans, dreams, and decisions get re-routed. We expend a lot of time and energy drawing up our plans, setting our goals, getting the education, and saving enough money to achieve our desires. Maybe you are a persistent planner like me, and you can surely relate to this scenario. Every Sunday evening, I map out my task list on my weekly planner. My kids think I'm over the top and cringe when they see my weekly planner spread out on the coffee table. They often wonder what's brewing for their next assignment and list of chores. But no matter how much I plan, there is often a delay or re-route. I'm pretty sure this happens to most of us, our plans are rarely smooth sailing and don't always turn out the way we intended. Re-routes can wreak havoc on our emotions if we aren't flexible and willing to adjust. Just as I questioned the logic and reasoning of Siri, I have questioned God at times about why my hard work of planning doesn't seem to be leading me to my desired destination. *Where are you God?* Have you been in that spot, questioning God in your re-route?

Trusting the Re-route

Trusting God in the re-route and embracing His change-of-plans is not an easy task. I want to be the director of my life. I prefer to control my route. But God warns us in Proverbs 3:5-6: "Trust in the Lord with all your heart and lean not on your own understanding; in all your ways submit to him, and he will make your paths straight." I love this analogy of a "straight path." It reminds me of driving up a mountain. I would rather my ascent be a straight, smooth path instead of curvy and winding. If you are prone to getting car sick, I am sure you would agree to forgo the winding road and drive a straighter path for your journey, too. A straight path doesn't impose as much danger as the winding road, so perhaps the benefits of trusting God seem reasonable. Trusting God is believing with all our heart that He knows best. It's exercising confidence that His path is safe, good, and long-lasting compared to our limited understanding. But that is difficult to grasp, especially if you are laid off from a job, not accepted into your school of choice, or delayed in your marriage plans or career. It's possible God may be directing you onto a different route, or simply causing you to acknowledge Him and submit to *His* understanding not your own. This is the hard work of faith.

Here's the truth I learned that day as I was late to my son's soccer tournament: When I choose to go my own way and not heed the warning, advice, or gentle whisper of the Holy

Spirit, my journey is often more difficult and painful. My stubborn and selfish ways can bellow impatience, causing more panic, frustration, and fear. I have come to realize, after resisting numerous re-routes, the Director (God) knows my destination better than I know it myself and I should listen to Him. The benefit is more peace and less strife when we listen to divine understanding. My understanding is imperfect, it can be easily broken, but His understanding never breaks, it is always secure, progressing at the opportune time. Basking in this truth has helped me to trust in the Lord and "lean not on my own understanding," especially in the re-route. As I learned from my experience with Siri, I hope you can also fathom how God is your perfect navigator and embracing His true understanding will always produce more benefit for you.

> *The hard work of faith is trusting in His understanding, not my own.*

Trusting in God's route is *Better Than Espresso*

Reflecting on Your Re-route

❖ Thinking about the Siri analogy, what plan of action did you put into place, but along the way you got re-routed?

❖ What did the re-route look like? Did you resist it at first?

❖ Looking back, was there a significant lesson you learned in the delay or re-route? How has this experienced shaped you?

Day 17

I'll Let Go of My Ideal
and Let God Lead

"And I am sure of this, that he who began a good work in you will bring it to completion at the day of Jesus Christ."
(Philippians 1:6 ESV)

Have you ever played tug-of-war and desperately wanted to let go of the rope? If you didn't let go, the sores on your hands could be more painful than the act of letting go and releasing the rope.

It was my son's sixth grade "Olympics" at school. The final event was tug-of-war and that year they decided to have the girls compete against the boys. The boys started off strong, motivated to show off their male power. They were not going to let the girls win!

Surprisingly, the boys lost. They gave a great effort and fight, but their strength dwindled, forcing them to let go of the rope. Imagine the embarrassment of sixth grade boys losing a physical game to sixth grade girls. Losing and letting go of the ideal is a blow to our pride.

Can you relate to those sixth-grade boys, you had to let go of an ideal you were holding firmly to? When your dream didn't come to fruition like you imagined? When your child disappointed you with the choices he or she made? When your Prince Charming and fairy tale marriage didn't end up as glamorous? I'm right there with you, girl. I too have struggled with my ideal life. Gripping tightly to our ideals is a real struggle and sometimes gives us rope burns. I had to learn a difficult lesson that started in my early young adult years, and continue to learn. It was to let go of what I thought my direction and plans was going to be, and start letting God lead it *His* way.

Benefits of Letting Go

Would you agree letting go is painful, especially if it is something we have a strong grip on? Letting go can emit feelings of loss and make us fear a dampened reputation. I can only imagine the sixth-grade boys feeling embarrassed by their loss to the girls. Their "tough" reputation was at stake. Have you had to release your grip on an image you were trying to protect? That's difficult, nobody wants their reputation damaged.

God reminds us, though, that His work is never done, even if our circumstance forced us to abandon our plans and our reputation suffered. He always completes His projects, and they are "immeasurably more than all we ask or imagine, according to his power that is at work within us" (Eph 3:20).

In that verse in Ephesians, Paul was reminding the Philippian church that they were doing good work. They needed this reminder because this was a time of great tension in the early church. Paul was also experiencing suffering as he wrote this letter from his prison cell. Life was hard for the Christians during the first century. But they learned that, as they let go of their ideal life, they found more joy and peace even in their suffering. Now that's a beautiful benefit that doesn't seem natural in the process of "letting go." Sometimes we just have to *let go, and let God*, then we find the joy and peace we have been looking for all along.

What are you gripping too tightly right now? Is there an ideal you're clenching which may be causing unrest in your direction and purpose? Maybe you are supposed to release this ideal because it has controlled you in more ways than one. I understand this emotion, I did not want to let go of my idealistic plans. But like the game of tug-of-war, I had to abandon my ideal because the rope burns were causing too much pain.

Why is it so important to learn how to let go? It builds our faith, character, and trust in God. Sounds so cliché, right? But here's the truth: We were not created to be in total control of our lives in the first place. Remember, He is God, not us! God will use the "thing" we grip, to help us grasp His faith and character of grace. Letting go is trusting His grip more than ours. It's not easy, it requires the supernatural. It's not possible to do this in our own strength. But again, God can do the *unimaginable* according to His power at work within us.

> *Letting go is trusting His grip more than ours.*

Visualize this imagery of release. You're flying in a plane or climbing up a steep mountain, moving your jaw endlessly to release the built-up pressure in your ears. There's no greater feeling than when your ears finally pop and release that pressure. Likewise, there is no greater feeling than when we release the pressure by loosening the grip that has a hold on us. In our *let go and let God* moments, something miraculous happens. Rope burns disappear, and greater joy and peace start to appear.

Letting go of the grip is *Better Than Espresso*

Reflecting on the *Let Go and Let God* Moments

❖ What is the game of tug-of-war you are playing right now that may be causing "rope burns"?

❖ Are you afraid to release the rope? _____ If so, what is making the release so difficult?

❖ What would it look like if you released the rope?

❖ What have you had to let go of in the past?

❖ Considering your answer to the question above, how did you see God complete a good work in your willingness to release?

Day 18

Being Comfortable with *Who* I am Allows Me to be Certain of *Where* I am Going

For you created my inmost being; you knit me together in my mother's womb.
I praise you because I am fearfully and wonderfully made;your works are wonderful, I know that full well.
(Psalm 139:13-14)

A re you someone who remembers your dreams? I don't usually remember my dreams, but there is one dream I have had since high school that re-occurs every so often. I wake up panicked, body in a cold sweat because I can't find my car. This dream always takes place at the mall parking structure. It's dark, I am alone carrying multiple bags, keys in hand, and I stop in my tracks staring at the parking structure ahead. Is my car on level one, two, or three? I wander aimlessly through the entire parking lot late at night looking lost and vulnerable. After searching all levels, I still can't find my car. Maybe I parked in the adjacent parking structure? Suddenly I wake up, heart beating faster than a high-speed chase wondering if I ever found my car.

The funny thing is, my dream has become reality, especially in my middle age. I kid you not, I walk out of stores more times than not questioning where I parked. One of my most embarrassing moments was walking out of a grocery market with two shopping carts filled to the brim wondering which aisle I had parked. Now here comes the embarrassing part; as I started walking down the aisles, I realized there were speed bumps and there was no alternative way to go around. Picture it for a moment, crazy lady with two huge shopping carts trying to go over speed bumps with groceries falling to the floor. It took me a few aisles before I found my car with sweat dripping down my bright red face.

Curiosity got the best of me now that my dream was becoming reality, so I decided to do a google search on dream analysis. Guess who popped right up? Dr. Oz so I decided to read what he had to say. This was my stress dream connected to uncertainty or loss of motivation. Wow now it all made sense. Uncertainty of parts of me has been a major theme I have had to battle for most of my life. I know Dr. Oz isn't God, but his description sure fit the picture.

Uncertainty Clouds Our Purpose

Uncertainty of self carries a lot of chaos and self-doubt. It impedes living out our passion and purpose well and our relationships can suffer too. A truth I believe is universal for most of us is; Being comfortable with WHO I am, allows me to be certain of WHERE I'm going. If you, like me, combat wondering thoughts about your purpose and direction, have there been detours, disappointments, or damaging words that cause you to question who you are? Do you struggle with jealousy or envy trying to live someone else's purpose? This can be easy to do when a friend receives a phone call for a job or awesome other opportunity she has dreamed. Everything seems to be falling into place for your friend, while your endeavors seem lifeless. Distractions of who we think we should be, and the direction our life should point, is a conduit to unsettledness. Here is a truth God is reminding me of; let go of who I am trying to be and embrace who GOD made me to be.

As you ponder the scripture above, visualize for a moment the word knit. What pops in your mind as you see this word? For me, I see my grandmother sitting on her distressed wooden rocking chair, knitting a pair of booties for her future grandchild. I imagine the big grin on her wrinkly face, excited and wondering what her grandchild will look like. She is thrilled to create a special piece of clothing that will protect her grandchild's feet from the cool breeze air. This visual is exactly who our God is. He knit you and I together with a unique piece of yarn, not the same as another. God had his hand over your mother's womb, he knew your personality, your strengths, how you were going to contribute to make a difference in this world. He also knew your weaknesses, your struggles and the pain you would endure. But the promise for ALL of us is, we are fearfully and wonderfully made, designed with his hand of protection even in our struggle. What is that struggle or disability that causes you feel so uncertain of who you are? How about if you looked at your trial differently and remember this:

Our biggest struggles become our biggest strengths, which become our greatest purpose.

Let's not allow our area of battle to define us and disrupt us from living out our God designed purpose. God is the author of our life, allowing us to see our creation as wonderful. As we become more intimate with the author of our life, we can move peacefully in our purpose.

> *Our biggest struggles become our biggest strengths, which become our greatest purpose.*

Embracing our design is *Better Than Espresso*

Reflecting on Being Comfortable with Yourself

❖ Take an honest assessment of yourself right now. What has caused you to not feel comfortable with *WHO* you are? (a situation, words from someone, disappointment)

❖ Psalm 139 says God knit you together fearfully and wonderfully. What is something unique about how you were knit together? (What is that unique yarn He used to design you?) Don't hold back, use the space below to record your unique strengths.

❖ Purpose is allowing your passions and strengths to collide. Take a moment to see if you can identify your purpose by completing the exercise below:
  - What is a passion that captivates your heart?

  - Considering the list of strengths you recorded above, write down some ideas of how you could use your strengths that are related to your passion:

  - My purpose Statement:
    I am passionate about:

    I will use my strength of (your top strength):

    To make a difference by:

Day 19

God Finds Me When I am Lost

"'For this my son was dead and is alive again; was lost and is found.' And they began to celebrate."
(Luke 15:22-24)

How do you react when you lose your phone? Does it send you into a frenzied panic?

We really *are* addicted to our technology, right?

My family was preparing to wind down for the evening and my youngest daughter panicked because her phone was nowhere in sight. She remembered holding it in her hand just 10 minutes ago, but suddenly it disappeared, vanished without any explanation. She searched high and low. The location of her phone became a mystery and soon the entire family was involved in the search for clues to find her missing phone.

After 10 minutes of retracing her steps (which seemed like an eternity), it dawned on us to look at the "Find My Friends" App. There it was, its location glaring right back at us on the screen. We headed toward the blue dot, but it was leading us to the front door. How could her phone be at this location, she never stepped a foot out the front door? After a few minutes of wresting and viewing the navigation, we realized her phone was located by the downstairs bathroom, which was near the front door. It was an exhausting search which required lots of patience, but in the end, so much celebration.

During the tiring search, I could see a look of hopelessness and despair in my daughter's face. She doubted her new phone would be found and the guilt of irresponsibility creviced in her heart. She was going to have to pay for a new phone if she had lost it.

Lost but Found

Just like losing a valued possession can cause turbulent moments, feeling a sense of loss in our purpose and circumstances can emit similar emotions. We can feel hopeless when our purpose seems cloudy and unclear. Purpose allows us to wake up excited, rejuvenated every day. It moves us and creates an opportunity for making a contribution to our world, and when we feel lost by it, it can be a very lonely and isolated place.

As women, you and I face many seasons in life – learning, school, work, building and reconstructing broken relationships, caring for children, caring for elderly parents, pursuing goals and dreams. But sometimes, our season of intent can feel disoriented, discontented, fragmented, and unclear. Transitions can surely disrupt our sense of purpose, leaving us directionless. Perhaps you are in a season like I am now – entering empty nest and wondering what is next. I never imagined this transition would feel so uncomfortable. Let's be real for a moment. It's easy to lose who we are as women when we are busy taking care of everyone else. Or maybe we have lost our sense of purpose and direction because in the depth of our souls, God is trying to do more. Perhaps there's a place of unforgiveness, wrongdoing, hurt, or shame He wants to reveal and then heal. That may be our intended purpose in the present moment, but we are fighting for more. God fully knows how our mistakes can entangle us and interrupt His pure design and purpose. His goal is for us to come to our spiritual senses and regroup the lost parts of our life.

The story of the prodigal son is found in the Bible. It is a life-changing story of one being lost, but then found. A father had two sons; the oldest who was fine with waiting for his father's inheritance, and the younger who wanted his share early so he could squander it. He was the prodigal son who wasted what was given to him. We don't know how he squandered it, but I would venture to say he engaged in a lot of mischievous behavior. Life became all about him. I can only imagine what a young man with an abundance of resources is tempted to do. Chasing down women, living in the moment with gluttony and foolishness, the worst kind of vices we can imagine. Now before you and I judge the prodigal son, we are just as guilty and ruthless. Our own follies may look different, but let's just name a few: willingly going against the wishes of God, selfish ambitions, envy and jealousy, lusts of desires and ambitions, constant discontent. Did the last one jump out at you like it did with me? I recognize how I have wasted valuable time and energy because I was not content. I sometimes want more of God's portion than what He has allotted to me in the moment. Discontent can be a catalyst for why we feel lost in our purpose and direction. Comparison, striving for selfish gain, pursuing wealth and pleasure often distract us from a deeper calling, and that is to serve others and not ourselves. As the story progresses, the younger son found himself driven to the ground. No more hope of being a prized citizen, but a servant who was deemed lower than the pigs (pretty bad!). No delicious food to eat and no friend or family to comfort and support him in his time of need. You could say he hit rock bottom and he knew it. He realized how far away from truth he had run. He was a lost soul, an undignified man because of his rebellion and desire to live life his way.

The good news is, he reclaimed himself and came to his senses. He realized and admitted his wrongdoing to his father. He desired a redeemed life, but with humility he didn't expect royal treatment from his father. A new heart allowed him to be content with the belief that he would be his father's servant, rather than his son. His mess-up led to so much misery, but his repentance is what led to his recovery. His father embraced his son's return and celebrated enormously. *My son was lost, but now is found.*

Can you identify with the prodigal son? Do you need to come to your senses and make a shift? Is there an area in your life causing you a sense of loss and a feeling of separation from the heart of God? Like the father in the story, our Heavenly Father reaches out His loving arms and extends a measure of grace and compassion when we tell Him we're sorry for going our own way. I admit, it can be difficult to accept, especially if our inner critic says we are not worthy of grace and compassion. But how long are we willing to live with a soul drenched in abandonment from a God who is waiting to celebrate us? When we apologize,

> *How long are we willing to live with a soul drenched in abandonment from a God who is waiting to celebrate us?*

admit, and return with humility, we are found again. Our purpose comes alive. God adorns us with honor and praise rather than guilt and defeat. His celebration redeems our lost portion. When my daughter found her phone, there was celebration and a sigh of relief and comfort. Likewise, when God finds us, he celebrates and creates a new version of us: A woman who is not lost in her purpose and in her circumstances, but a woman found with fierce and unique passion.

Reclaiming what's been lost, is
Better Than Espresso

Reflecting on Being Found

❖ Losing our phones can feel detrimental because they have unfortunately become our livelihood and even a prized possession. What is something tangible and of value that you lost -- either temporarily (like not being able to find your ring or phone or child for a time) or permanently (like money, a house, or something else of value)?

❖ What are some intangible losses that have occurred in your life? (purpose, title, position, status, relationship, job/ career, reputation)

❖ What emotions were associated with losing the tangible or intangible losses?

❖ How did you experience God's tenderness during your season of loss?

❖ The Prodigal son was lost and isolated from his family because of his choices. *But his repentance led to a life of recovery.* If you have isolated your heart from God, what would a life of recovery look like for you if you invited him back? Think about these examples for your own life.
  - God extending undeserving grace and compassion .
  - Excited about your new-found passion and purpose.
  - Celebration of a new you. A spirit of gratitude instead of grudges.
  - A new marriage built on a firmer foundation.
  - A restored relationship with a child or friend.
  - A positive and growing mindset.

God is waiting to find you again my friend. He loves you that much!

Day 20

Training Prepares Me
for the Win

*"Do you not know that in a race all runners run,
but only one gets the prize? Run in such a way
as to get the prize. Everyone who competes in
the games goes into strict training. They do it
to get a crown that will not last; but we do it to
get a crown that lasts forever."*
(1 Corinthians 9:24-25)

I get exhausted by *trying* to make things happen in my life.
Trying to find my purpose, *trying* to stay in shape and eat-
ing healthy, *trying* to stay positive when my mind fights
the negative, *trying* to have a better relationship with my husband and kids, *trying* to save more rather than spend. TRY,
TRY, TRY!

For most of us, it was ingrained in us as children to *try
harder* when circumstances didn't go our way. In school, it

was common to hear, "try harder." On the field, coaches are yelling from the sidelines, "ramp up your game, try harder." I don't know if you have had similar thoughts, but sometimes the more I seem to try without the proper training, the more I am set up for disappointment. Can you relate?

Think about it. It's risky for an athlete to walk onto the field or platform without stretching and training for a specific skill. Imagine a coach of an Olympic gymnastics team telling the girls to try their best, but not putting into practice a rigorous training program. I am quite certain the gymnasts would be very discouraged by their high-level routines on a 4-inch beam. It is imperative for any athlete to train their body well for competition. If not, the body is likely to break down with serious injury. If we just have the mindset to try harder without putting into action a training routine, I think we would both agree defeat is around the corner. I surely don't want to live my life feeling defeated, and I'm positive neither do you.

The Benefit of Training

As Paul drew the parallel in 1 Corinthians 9:25-26, *strict training* is necessary to win a prize in athletic games, as well as in our spiritual life. Winning a race takes determination and discipline. But running the race in the Christian life is not about winning a prize for the moment. No, Paul is trying to discipline our minds toward the attributes of Christ because they matter more and are everlasting compared to winning the race of the world. Training to forgive your betrayer is not easy. Training to love the unlovable requires compassion. Training to live out your purpose when the losses are more than the wins requires divine endurance. A better heart instead of a bitter heart, compassion, and endurance are outpourings of our spiritual equipping. Training as opposed to trying often leaves us with more stamina, personal growth, and better results. Our purpose usually becomes clarified in our training as well.

It takes practice and a special kind of endurance to win. As a mom of three athletic children, I know this truth quite well. I remember one moment when my daughter was chosen to take a penalty kick for her soccer team to win the game. Talk about pressure. I was so nervous for her because I know what pressure does to her. But I had to remind myself that she had been training for moments like this. She paused for a moment, focused on what she needed to do, said a quick prayer, prepared her stance, and kicked the black and white ball fiercely into the net. She kicked the winning goal and mama's lungs exploded all over the field.

It was her training that prepared her for the win.

I recently hosted a guest on my podcast who shared a couple thoughts from her book *Show Up for Your Life*. Here are a couple of quotes from Crystal Evans Hurst:[1]

"Unhealthy emotions are indicators to retrain."

"Truth should drive our emotions."

"Much of our success is moved by the smaller steps."

When my emotions slap me across the face, it signals to me that I need better training. Speaking kindly instead of condemning myself has been my marathon of a run. I have tried endlessly to fix myself. With God's help and His perspective, I am learning the required strategy to train my emotions for a healthier mind. It surely requires the intention and self-discipline, but the reward is we handle ourselves better in the game of life. Do you have an area in your life where practice may be required for some refining?

Paul was urging us to develop a training mindset, an eternal mindset, a mindset of faith, rather than become stuck in the world's attitude of *try harder*. There is an enormous difference between trying and training. Trying is fleeting, it caters to our flesh. We can become more susceptible to moving from one thing to the next without landing anywhere. Have you witnessed this in your own life? The course you set out for yourself gets disrupted because you just keep trying to make it happen without the required training needed? Discontentment enters the scene and you are never fulfilled with your God-designed purpose and plan. But when we train God's way, we win. We do not give up because He helps us build an endurance that lasts in the difficult moments! If we yield to our flesh, we lose, and it always poses a danger to give up. But when you press forward your purpose starts to unveil because you see the bigger picture of running the race with a different perspective: *training vs. trying.* Training God's way conditions our souls so that we are more fruitful in our values, dreams, and God-given opportunities. I consider this a *big* win, don't you?

Training in our faith is *Better Than Espresso*

Reflecting on the "Train Well" Moments

❖ Describe an area of your life in which you keep *trying,* but you are not seeing satisfying results.

❖ Now, take a moment for some personal inventory. In understanding a trying-versus-training mindset, how would you rate yourself in the following areas? Are you stuck in your trying or are you developing a training mindset?

Marriage:	Trying_____	Training_____
Relationship w/Kids:	Trying_____	Training_____
Eating Right:	Trying_____	Training_____
Friendships:	Trying_____	Training_____
Work/ Career:	Trying_____	Training_____
Finances:	Trying_____	Training_____
Faith:	Trying_____	Training_____
Hobbies:	Trying_____	Training_____
Time Management:	Trying_____	Training_____

❖ For the areas you marked *Trying*, what are some practical steps you can take to begin training? (i.e. pray for husband, hug your kids even when they don't deserve, listen better, develop a budget, spiritual meditation)

❖ For the areas you marked *Training*, what are the disciplines you have developed to get you into this mindset?

Great job my friend, keep going.

Part 5

When Your Identity is Threatened

Day 21

Changing My Perspective Changes My Posture

Do not conform to the patterns of this world, but be transformed by the renewing of your mind. Then you will be able to test and approve what God's will is—his good, pleasing and perfect will.
(Romans 12:2)

Have you ever been among a group of women and experienced the feeling that you didn't belong? Perhaps at *one time* you felt you belonged, but then you began to question it.

That happened to me. As each woman around the table was celebrating God's work in her life, I felt uneasy and insecure because, at that moment, it was difficult for me to see how God was moving in *my* life. I anxiously tried to pull something out of my magical hat, looking for some words of acceptance. But, I didn't feel the love. In fact, I felt like the child at school who was pushed out of line.

How my heart breaks when I see children get pushed out of line when they are simply trying to fit in with their classmates in order to feel a sense of belonging. Our sinful nature is bullying at times.

My problem that day around the table with the women was that my perspective needed to change. Perspective is about seeing something from a larger frame of reference and I could only see what my emotions were dictating to me. I felt out of place at that table and believed I didn't belong because my viewpoint was that *they* were moving forward, and I was not. My limited perspective was not helping my posture of insecurity.

Renew the Mind

Paul, believed to be the writer of Romans, knew from personal experience the importance of renewing the mind. It changes our perspective. Paul understood our human condition of desiring to conform to the patterns of the world:

We want to be first in line.

We need to feel important and valued by others.

We long to look good to everyone around us.

We have an insatiable need to feel loved and desired.

Romans 12:2 – which tells us not to conform to the patterns of this world, but to be renewed by the *transforming* of our minds – gives us a framework for helping us change our perspective when it has gone askew. The truth is, when our limited perspective begins to shift into a positive direction, our posture starts improving.

As the evening progressed at that gathering of women, God quickly nipped my posture (of feeling *out* of place) *into* place. He reminded me of the good work He is doing of renewing my mind – destroying the jealousies in my spirit, the comparisons that bring me down, and my need to impress others. He gave me a gift that evening as the women were taking turns sharing their thoughts. I heard His gentle whisper on my heart: *Julie, you are not being shoved out of line. I have a special place in line for you, but it's going to be a little while longer. Hang on to My truths, keep your mind renewed, resist the thoughts of your adversary, and soon enough your place will be revealed.*

As I laid my head down on my pillow that evening, I surrendered to the God who can renew my mind and change my perspective. Instead of waking up the next morning with a posture of defeat, I rose with an invigorated posture – with shoulders back, head held high, ready to face the day with new opportunity and adventure from my God.

Do *you* need a change of perspective, so your posture can be positive as opposed to negative? What practices are you putting into place to help you renew your mind? Are there areas where you need to die to your sinful desires so there can be a conversion of perspective? This is not an easy task, but the more we practice renewing our minds in Christ Jesus, the flesh (which manifests itself in jealousy, comparison, discontent) minimizes. When these fleshly attitudes decrease, we become women who can stand tall and proclaim, "God is doing great things in me, too."

The best part about our new perspective is that we become available to the next woman in line who has been shoved, left out, and uninvited. You can help change *her* posture and by doing so, find much joy.

A healthy perspective is *Better Than Espresso*

Reflecting on Your Perspective

❖ Would you consider your overall perspective about your life positive or negative and why?

❖ Describe what has influenced your perspective (your upbringing, successes, failures, disappointments):

❖ Your posture for the day is influenced by your perspective. Renewing the mind can change your perspective and start your day off right. See if you can identify with these examples of disciplining and renewing the mind:
  - Talk to yourself with compassion instead of condemnation.
  - Dispose the jealousy toward your friend and celebrate her success.
  - Train your mind to stay in your lane and not be conformed to the enticing messages by the world.

- Read God's Word first thing in the morning to fill your mind with faith instead of fear.
- Allow God to transform your life, not just improve it.
- Take every lie and false belief captive, and hand it over to the one (God Almighty) who can distinguish them and feed your mind with truth.

❖ If you would like a tool to help renew your mind daily, check out my removable/ non-adhesive mirror decals on my website that reflect truths instead of lies. Place these on your morning mirror and recite and repeat these truths. You will be amazed how your posture starts changing when you feed your mind with core truths. Again you can find mirror decals at my website.

https://juliepearson.org/shop

Day 22

Attach Value to My "Who," Not My "Do"

But the LORD said to Samuel, "Do not look on his appearance or on the height of his stature, because I have rejected him. For the LORD sees not as man sees: man looks on the outward appearance, but the LORD looks on the heart."
(1 Samuel 16:7)

"What was the score?"

I'm guilty of saying that and maybe you are, too. As a mom of three driven athletes, this is common language in my household. But lately I want to be more cautious about the rhetoric I use with my children. Instead of asking, "What was the score?" I want my first response to be "How did you feel about your game?" Why is this question more important than the first? It creates a dialogue for our kids to engage more intimately, instead of stopping with a one-sentence response: "The score was 2-3." Whether you have children in sports or not, how you ask questions, and how they answer, may provide insight into how your kids primarily define their value – by their scorecard or who they are as a created human being.

I share this thought because I can easily attach my value and identity to my scorecard. In the past few years, I have found a new love in the sport of tennis. Hitting that small fluorescent ball over the net is more challenging than you think, especially if you possess a competitive spirit like mine. Tennis is really a frustrating sport and I have noticed how it can beat me up at times. (Now I understand why a boy I dated in high school had a temper on the tennis court.) My husband has graciously agreed to play tennis with me on the weekends to help me gain more practice. Why did I agree to this? I am a glutton for punishment. He *always* wins, and it frustrates me to no end. I am the one taking lessons, so you would think my scorecard would outshine his, but it never does. I have walked off the tennis court numerous times beating myself up over a leisurely game. "I always lose." "I'm no good." "I don't measure up." Those were the false narratives in my mind not only on the tennis court, but in other areas of my life as well. I often find my value in my scorecard, and that can be a detriment to my identity because I can't always win.

Constantly measuring our performance against the world's scorecard will eventually suck us dry. Think about how you feel after scrolling through social media for long periods of time. Does it suck you in like a vacuum and then leave you with murky thoughts? If we aren't using it carefully, it can be a platform of damaging messages and an inaccurate measure of "who" we are. Don't you think there is a wiser method of forming our worth and value as opposed to grading ourselves on how the world defines us? I don't know about you, but I get exhausted in trying to keep up with a scorecard to impress the world. I think God has better answers for us. When we put our faith and trust in the divine, we begin to see an evolution take place with our own mindsets. We start to see God's economy of value shaping our lives, as opposed to the broken world's economy. He says our value as human beings is in our hearts not our heads. Let's unpack this for a moment because it can be so contrary to how we feel.

Our Value is More Than a Scorecard

Samuel was a high-profile judge in the Old Testament. He was assigned a divine task – to anoint a new king over Israel. God was displeased with Saul, the current king. God wanted a king who sought after His own heart. In 1 Samuel 16, God told Samuel to visit the seven sons of Jesse. Among them was an appointed man that God had chosen to be king. Samuel thought it was Jesse's first son because he appeared to be king-like, tall in stature. But God said he wasn't the one. "The Lord does not look at things man looks at." As the story unfolds, Samuel was told by God to anoint the youngest son as king. David was small in stature, not kinglike, just a small, simple, shepherd boy. I'm sure questions whirled around in Samuel's mind. *How could this simple boy be the anointed king?* But, God's economy is different than man's economy. David, whose name means "beloved," was divinely anointed as Israel's king not because of his outward appearance, but because of who he was on the inside. God reminds us in this story that His favor and honor is often given to those who have been least regarded by the world.

What about you? Were you chosen for a promotion despite your performance not measuring up like expected? That is unwarranted favor and it reveals this truth – performance does not determine our value. Or, perhaps you constantly feel discouraged because you have allowed your scorecard to define your who. If so, keep the story of David close to your heart. I admit, it's in our human nature to derive a sense of value from our achievements. But performance can be short-lived, altered at any moment (like the stock market), so it's not a reliable benchmark upon which to determine our value. If your emotions are negatively affected by your scorecard, maybe it's an opportunity to reassess how your identity is defined. Is it defined by what you do, how much you accomplish, your successes, applause and approval from the rest of the world? If so, you are going to live in constant exhaustion trying to keep up.

I have had to learn to re-define expectations of myself and not base them on my scorecard. Just the other day, I had to do this while playing tennis with my husband. I deliberately didn't allow myself to be consumed by the score (truthfully, I really wanted to beat him), but I was focused more on my own game. Friend, I was losing big time, but I switched my mindset in the middle of the game. I stayed calm, remained positive, and focused on how I could improve my next shot, instead of feeling defeated by my performance. It worked... I came back after losing three games in a row. My husband ultimately won the match, but I walked off the court praising my comeback, instead of my performance labeling my worth.

As I walked off the court, I realized that if I focus too much on my scorecard and allow it to determine my value, I sabotage myself. If I can't be at ease with myself, that's when my game (on and off the court) usually suffers. My identity continues to be threatened if I depend on the world to tell me my score, instead of surrendering to God's economy of scoring.

Here are some practical lessons from tennis that apply to our everyday lives:

- Compete with yourself more than others.
- Tell yourself how *you* can do better, rather than focus on how your opponent did better.
- Focus on improvement, more than judgment.
- Attach your value to your "who" more than your "do."
- Your heart – how you treat others, and how you love God and yourself, matters more than your appearance and applause.
- You will gain more respect from people when your value is shaped by authentic concern for others.
- Remember, friend, our intrinsic value is not driven by our performances (which are inconsistent), but by the health of our souls.

Our "Who" is *Better Than Espresso*

Reflecting on Your Value

❖ Take a look at your own scorecard. Answer the following questions as honestly as you can and give each a score as follows: 1= Least likely; 2 = Likely; 3= Most likely

1) I pay more attention to my strengths than my weaknesses _____

2) I value my strengths and how I contribute to society _____

3) I learn from my failures/ mistakes and evaluate how I can do better next time_____

4) When I complete a project or assignment, I often feel good about my work even if others did a better job_____

5) I receive constructive feedback well _____

6) I start the day off with a positive thought about God or myself and how I contribute _____

7) I am pleased with what I have accomplished in life so far_____

8) I am thankful for how God created me, strengths, weaknesses and all _____

9) I am not focused on my performance and how I am doing to impress others. I just focus on doing my best_____

10) I find it more important to be defined by my character more than my performance and accomplishments

_____

TOTAL SCORE:_____

Score of 25+: You place more value in your "who" that what you do. Great job.

Score of 15-24: Your scorecard needs some adjustments. You may be too focused on your performance rather than who you are as a person.

Score 3-14: Your value is apparently dependent on your scorecard. Practice showing more "kindness" to yourself.

❖ David was chosen for his "who" not his "do" nor his appearance. Do you have a picture of your "who?" What does that look like and how does it make you valuable to the world?

Day 23

Progress Comes
When I Plug into My
God-Given Power

For the Spirit God gave us does not make us
timid, but gives us power, love and self-disci-
pline.
(2 Timothy 1:7)

I allowed doubt to settle in my mind and it unplugged my power.

I was recently talking with a dear friend who is accomplishing great things in her ministry. When we are together, it's a sweet time of sharing our praises and disappointments. Friends are a true gift from God, especially the ones who can build us up. I hope you have a friend who encourages your life when it takes a U-turn.

I was sharing with my friend a desire placed in my heart, but doubt and fear locked up this desire. I didn't have anything left in me to keep going. I lost all power within myself, which threatened my sense of identity. She looked straight into my eyes with confident conviction and said, "Julie, you need to stand in your power."

Immediately tears streamed down my face. I broke down, my spirit overwhelmed. I was in a season of loss, how could I possibly "stand" in my power? She reminded me that I was relying on my own inner strength which was depleting me, but there was a different power source available if I just learned to tap into it. I knew exactly what she was talking about. I have been in church my whole life. She was referring to *God's* power – the power of the Holy Spirit. But I had lost all confidence in God; I felt forgotten by Him.

The Right Source of Power

Have you ever felt forgotten by God? Have you been unsure about the power Paul talks about in the verse referenced above? I agree it's difficult to comprehend that God does not give us a spirit of timidity when we are in a place consumed by our fears, challenges, and disappointments. Fighting our fears of the flesh is a constant battle. I find myself giving into my flesh more than obeying my spirit. It's a difficult process relying on and trusting in God's sovereignty. My pride constantly fights to be the one who is capable.

After the conversation with my dear friend, I departed with an overwhelming sense of assurance I haven't felt in a long time. As long as I tap into the power of the Holy Spirit (which is a continual process) I will make progress. I had one of those mascara-all-over-my-face, sobbing cry sessions while driving home. I'm sure the drivers around me were nervous about what I might do while driving in such an emotional frenzy. I was finally agreeing with God that His Spirit allows me the ability to stand confidently when it seems unattainable. He quietly whispered to my heart, *Julie, I will give you the courage to progress and face your fears and failures. I will give you the power to re-live your dream and live your purpose. Place your trust in Me because I am the author of courage, not cowardice and slavish fears.* Isn't it wonderful that when we cry out to God He shows up with a gentle whisper? It makes the mascara-smearing, cry session all worth it!

My hope is you, too, begin tapping into the power source of God, erasing the ferocious fear and timidity that is holding you back from your dream, purpose, and passion. *Progress is possible if you plug into the right power source.* Removing distractions keeps the power surge strong. Our distractions may include:

- Promises of wealth if you invest in that next self-help book.
- Guaranteed beauty if you buy the latest skin product.
- Success in the marketplace if you cheat, lie, or dress more expensively.
- Pressure or a sense of competition to look and act like the successful person you admire.

These are also outside voices distracting our progress and threatening our identity, and we need to learn to fight against that artificial power. Standing in your God-given power is not being fixated on how your neighbor is succeeding in life, but behaving with complete assurance that God has favor for you, too. It may look different, but the temptation to compare depletes your ability to *stand in your God-given power.*

When God is our mentor, our stance is more resolute, our progress is more assured. No one is immune from hardships, even though the world will have us think differently. As you and I learn the secret of our internal power, it will be attractive to your next friend or family member who experiences suffering and calamity. God loves it when we proclaim His power and give it away. Plugging into the correct source of power not only gives us progress, but equips us to battle the fears that threaten our well-being. God's power is our ultimate sustainer; it keeps our minds steady, sound, strong, and still.

> *God loves it when we proclaim His power and give it away.*

Spiritual power is *Better Than Espresso*

Reflecting on Your Power

❖ Think about a power source (plugging into an electric outlet, booting up your computer or charging your iphone). What benefits do we derive from plugging into a power source?

❖ Reflect on your current journey. Are you seeing any of these benefits displayed in your life? If not, why not?

❖ Can you identify your sources of distraction that keep you from plugging into the right power source? (comparison, worldly opinions, temptations)

❖ If your identity is weakened, maybe it's time for you to plug into the right power source. Remember God doesn't give you a spirit of timidity. When you plug into Him, your power surges. What would this new surge of power look like for you? How would you be different?

Day 24

My Hacker Intrudes,
but
My God Renews

"Before I formed you in the womb I knew you,
before you were born I set you apart;
I appointed you as a prophet to the nations."
(Jeremiah 1:5)

H ave you ever had your phone or computer hacked?
While I was enjoying a once-in-a-lifetime opportunity to visit Israel, my phone got hacked. It was a
scary experience because unfamiliar people had access to my
personal information. In today's world of technology, hack-
ers are on the rise trying to steal our identity and all that we
have.

In the spiritual world, there also exists a hacker. As a Christ-follower who places God at the center of her life, I am aware there is an adversary who is against me. He wants to steal and destroy every part of me. Our adversary is like a prowling lion seeking whom he can devour. (1 Peter 5:8) And Jesus said the enemy has come to kill, steal and destroy. (John 10:10) Satan's desire is to hack those things near and dear to my heart. That is his best method to keep me from following the author of my life, Jesus Christ.

My identity (who I am, what I do, how I contribute) is one of the areas I hold close to my heart. I can honestly admit my identity is one of my earnest battles with the enemy. He knows it is an opportune place to intrude because I inadvertently place much significance in my title, assignments, purpose, and accomplishments.

Just like I experienced a phone hacker in Israel, there lies a hacker in my soul. It was a few years ago, my hacker tried to steal my sense of identity. My once-pronounced labels were removed, like the old tattered jean labels that get destroyed in the wash. I no longer possessed a label that I felt distinguished myself. That was difficult, especially for a girl who likes the labels on her designer jeans! Those labels (physical and emotional) comforted me, they told me who I was and identified me to the world.

It took some time to recover from my intruder's assault. It was a season when God was doing His best work in me, restoring and renewing my lost identity. I began to see the truth behind today's verse. *God formed me in my mother's womb and created me to be set apart.* I realize this concept may be

> **My hacker may try to mess up my assignments, but God will always clean them up.**

difficult for you to grasp as it is for me. But when God transformed me, I began to see the principle behind this verse. God formed me to be set apart for various unique assignments and it's through my life's journey that these assignments are discovered. My hacker may try to mess them up, but my God will always clean them up!

When the Hacker Intrudes

Jeremiah was a prophet who was appointed (set apart) to do the hard work of bringing God's people back to restoration. Jeremiah didn't think his character matched up to the assignment. He saw himself differently and didn't desire the appointment. However, it was in his own journey with God that he became fortified for the task and equipped to withstand the intruders he would encounter. He discovered that his true identity was not in his own strengths and abilities, but leaning into *who* God appointed him to be, and noticing the signs confirming his assignment.

Have you experienced a similar story in which your identity was challenged? Maybe you lost a job you absolutely loved, and the title on your business card was suddenly removed. Or maybe your role as Mom of the Year was challenged. Perhaps your bank account that labeled you a success has just been bankrupt. Those circumstances can disrupt our existence and test our personal status. If our identity is not secure in the living God who created us and set us apart, then it can be devastating when our hacker intrudes. We will feel robbed of our titles, achievements, and progress and it can wreak havoc on our life. Perhaps it's time for us to get fortified like Jeremiah, so when challenges come, we are ready to ascertain the truth because we know who we are.

I knew it was necessary for me to surrender my labels and image management because my identity was dependent on them. It was a very painful, but needed process, so God could rebuild my charred self. I had to abandon the labels I thought completed me. Finally, I had to start anticipating new gifts for my next God assignment. When you and I surrender our status and symbols the blessings become more abundant. They are more than we imagined. God gifted me the other day through a woman who reminded me how important the labels God had assigned to me and confirmed that I have been "set apart." I walked away blessed by her comment, placing my full confidence in the fact that God identifies me, not the hacking attempts by my enemy. The next time you experience a hack to your identity, remain fortified in these two truths:

You are not defined by your titles, positions, or achievements. Let go of those labels so you can move into your God-appointed assignments.

You were formed in the womb, created to be set apart, using your God given skills, abilities, and strengths to bless someone else, not to glorify self.

Surrendering our labels is *Better Than Espresso*

Reflecting on Your Identity

❖ Be honest with yourself. What are the labels you own that give you a sense of stability and identity?

❖ Imagine those labels completely removed from your life. Take an honest inventory and reflect how this would affect your identity, security and sense of self-worth? Is there evidence that you allow your labels to determine who you are?

❖ If your identity has been hacked take a good look at Jeremiah chapter 1 in the Old Testament. Pause and reflect these words carefully. Notice how God set you apart. He appointed you for a special purpose to be a difference maker. When we can see our lives as appointed and set apart, that's when our identity comes alive. You matter my friend!

Day 25

Filter Old Thoughts to Make Room for the New

Therefore, if anyone is in Christ, the new creation has come: The old has gone, the new is here!
(2 Corinthians 5:17)

My new refrigerator just arrived. After it was hooked up, I couldn't wait to dump the old one and have a new fresh place to store my food. I was excited to pour myself a glass of ice-cold water from the new water filter. I grabbed the glass on the counter and pressed the button. *Yuck!* The water that poured out of the spout looked like something I would find in our rain gutter! I didn't realize there was a necessary filtering process before we could enjoy fresh water from our new fridge.

We had to pour out at least a gallon of residue water before we could enjoy the good, new fresh water. As I stood in my kitchen enduring this process, it provided a great visual for me. I desire a great marriage with my husband, healthy relationships with my kids, a purposeful future, and a strong identity. But, if there is residue built up in my life, it must be filtered. Unhealthy habits, mindsets, attitudes, and beliefs must be filtered out to make room for the new. Otherwise, the old and unfiltered will continue to contaminate the new.

> *The old and unfiltered will continue to contaminate the new.*

Filtering Allows for the New

Second Corinthians 5:17 says "if anyone is in Christ, the new creation has come: The old has gone, the new is here!" That verse makes a very clear point. For transformation to happen, it's not about the other person or circumstance changing. It's about us changing, especially our mindsets which carry a lot of weight in polluting our thoughts. What does that look like? Honestly, it's about looking inside ourselves and noticing unhealthy patterns of thinking, habits that may indicate a hint of laziness. It's about becoming aware of our tone of voice when speaking to our husbands and children. It involves choosing healthy relationships instead of unhealthy ones, and making good choices in our diet and extracurricular activities. This is all well and good, but let's get real for a minute. It's an enduring process to filter out the pollutants. It requires time, patience, and prayer is not a bad idea either.

But girlfriend, it is possible for you and me to filter our fruitless, habitual, and damaging thoughts. It's about being disciplined in the moment and exercising a filtering strategy. For example, when an adverse thought surfaces your mind, such as, "I'm not worthy", test it. Immediately combat it with an absolute truth~ *God loves me and designed me, so that makes me worthy.* Learning to dispute the adverse thought says, "I'm learning to see myself differently." As our relationship with Christ grows, he makes this process easier. His truths are far greater than our own perceptions of truth. We can't do it on our own merit. I think it's interesting how we are commanded to renew our minds and not our bodies. God must have known that our biggest battle is with our mind and thoughts (which impacts the soul and spirit), not our bodies.

I'm so glad I have a partner (God) to help me become a better version of myself. We are new creations when we put our lives in God's hands. My thoughts need filtering quite often, and God reminds me when they need to be changed. Imagine if we never cleaned our pool or air conditioning filters. Not only would there be disgusting residue, but the equipment wouldn't run as efficiently. It works the same for you and me. If too much residue resides in our thoughts, we are not going to be our best versions of ourselves My unfiltered mind can easily threaten my identity with false beliefs and narratives. I can easily conform to the world's pattern of thinking. I like what it initially has to offer – status, security, and popularity. That is why I absolutely need my sticky quotes to keep my mind from conforming to the old patterns of thinking. If you are trying to renew your mind with a positive mindset, it may require you to limit your time with the naysayers. You may need to say no to an activity or a person for some time, to allow your brain to be conditioned for the new. And you may need to spend more time in God's Word than listening to the advice out in the world.

Filtering out the old to achieve the new has great benefits. The new, clean water from my fridge is a prime example. Like filtered water, we become a changed person. Our potential starts to increase, and our dreams come alive. The silt that once caused a lot of heartache, filters out to leave us with clean hearts and minds. That struggling relationship doesn't seem to be as difficult. The better version of you probably diffuses a lot of unnecessary arguments. Your reactions are better managed and controlled. I'm sure your husband, kids, or boss can appreciate the new you. Your better version allows your mind to be more positive rather than negative, creating greater opportunity and more creativity. We just can't beat the benefits! It's well worth the process of "being a new creation" and filtering the old to make room for the new.

A filtered mind is *Better Than Espresso*

Reflecting on Filtering Out the Old

❖ Using the refrigerator example, identify some residue that needs to be filtered from your life. Briefly describe what this residue looks like.

❖ What does transformation (or a new creation) look like for you?

❖ Identify one polluted thought and try this exercise as a starting place to filter:

- My polluted thought is?

- What is a truth to counter this polluted thought?

- Dispute the polluted thought (what are you learning that counters this adverse thought?)?

- What is your new healthy thought?

Part 6

When You're Changed by God's Character

Day 26

God's Not Finished
with Me Yet

For I know the plans I have for you," declares
the LORD, *"plans to prosper you and not to harm
you, plans to give you hope and a future. Then
you will call on me and come and pray to me,
and I will listen to you. You will seek me and
find me when you seek me with all your heart.*
(Jeremiah 29:11-13)

She was a stay-at-home mom married for 10 years when her husband suddenly walked out. She was left with two young children feeling insecure, unstable, and uncertain about her future. Her husband didn't want to work on the marriage – he was done, finished, and moved on. Meanwhile, she was trying to pick up the shattered pieces, but she couldn't. Her happily-ever-after wasn't so happy. In fact, her dismantled marriage threw her into a sea of depression. With no strength to face the day, she found herself stuck in bed. Hope eluded her. As the days passed, it became more difficult for her to prop her head up from the pillow, swirl her legs to the side of the bed, plant her feet on the ground, and give herself a morning welcome in her bathroom mirror. Instead, her head and body stayed tucked in her cozy linen sheets, which became her new normal. Days became weeks with more anger brewing toward her husband. It all culminated into a night she would never forget. All alone, she collapsed onto her bathroom floor and cried out to her Abba Father: "Why is this happening? Where are You in my pain?"

I have been there before and maybe you have, too. Life can take a sudden U-turn, and it can become so paralyzing. In one of my darkest hours, I couldn't get the raving thought out of my mind, *God's done with me, I no longer have a bright future ahead.* My friend had these same thoughts. In her dreary moment on the floor, bathed in tears and with no more tissues, she suddenly felt an overwhelming peace flood through her body. A sweet tender "touch from Heaven" assured her heart as her heavenly Father whispered, "You are not alone My child, I will be by your side because I'm not finished with you yet." These were the comforting words her heart needed to hear because her spirit had been consumed with uncertainty and fear of the unknown.

Today my friend is certain of God's faithfulness that picks us up after our desperate cries for help, hope, and answers. She is confident that God isn't finished with any of us yet. You may be lying prostrate on your bathroom floor today because of loss and hardship. God's not finished with *you* yet, either. Or, maybe you have recently come through a dark season, and now you can celebrate and validate this same thought. Hopefully you are willing to share this message with those who currently see the floor more than the sky.

God is Faithful

Jeremiah was one of God's greatest prophets (and voices of the Lord) in the Old Testament. It's fascinating to read about people like him who long ago had a message, and it relates to us today. He wrote a letter to God's people who were exiled by the kingdom of Babylon because they chose to go their own way. Consequently, the Israelites thought God had forgotten about them. They were no longer living in the comfort of their own land. But Jeremiah's message was clear, God had not forsaken them. In fact, God provided a lot of good in their captive land. They were encouraged by Jeremiah to seek the good, even when the good was not visible. God continued to show favor on His people, despite their exile. They were given comforting shelter, food, and continued to enjoy the great celebrations of life like marriage and family. However, they could only see uncertainty, wondering if the opportunity would arise for them to migrate back to their land of comfort and security. Jeremiah's job was to deliver a life-changing message. God was not finished with them if they sought Him with all their hearts. There were plans in the making for their bright and hopeful future. One day they would be gathered back to their original land. The Israelites eventually were freed from exile, but not without patience, surrender, and God's perfect timing. Our own stories breed fear, doubt and uncertainty for our future. We, too, may view God as against us, not for us. But like my friend who cried out to Him on her bathroom floor, you can be assured that God is faithful, working behind the scenes to mend what appears to be a broken future.

After a few years of allowing God's divine healing, the broken marriage that left my friend alone and scared on her bathroom floor, became "the better plan." She and her husband both realized God wasn't finished with their marriage. Through hard work, prayer, and diligence on both parties, their marriage was reconciled. As Jeremiah encouraged, they sought the good, even when the good was not visible. Compassion was a result of seeking the good. My friend described her prayer during one of her private moments: "God break me for what breaks Your heart." She can now sit with others who are in pain because God gave her a new heart of compassion. There is beauty in our moments of vulnerability. Her reformed identity became the jewel found in a treasure chest. Before her marriage crisis, she described herself as co-dependent, not knowing her individual voice. She relied mostly on her husband's voice, which contributed to issues in her marriage. Courage became her strength and it literally allowed her to soar. (In fact, she bravely parachuted out of a plane recently as a symbol of freedom and soaring above her fears.) She went back to school and learned new skills and talents that helped her gain a new sense of identity. No longer dependent on her husband to satisfy her life, she is now surrendered to God.

If crises and difficulties cause you to question if God is finished with you, take a moment and pause. Converse with God: "Teach me to seek You. Help me see Your faithfulness. Will You confirm how this plan is to prosper me, not harm me?" We must remember as His beloved ones, He moves *toward* us with love and mercy, not away from us. It may seem like He is distant in your moment of crisis, but mercy is His preference. Like a mom who loves her child, God wants the best for His children. My friend now sees the building block of faith because of her painful moments. As I write this chapter, her faith is being tested again with a current job layoff and financial uncertainty. But she places her hope and future not in today's circumstance, but in tomorrow's plan. She survived deep waters in the past, and it gives her more hope and assurance that God will save her again.

God is not finished with you yet, either (even if your marriage is in crisis and doesn't turn out like my friend's). He is faithful. Keep seeking Him. God is working behind the scenes to mold you, mature you, and present a platter of "plans to prosper you, not harm you."

God's plans are *Better Than Espresso*

Reflecting on God's Faithfulness

❖ How can you relate to my friend's story? Is there a scenario (either current or past), where you have felt distant from God? Write about this scenario in the space below.

❖ If God hasn't been a part of your life, what holds you back from believing in Him? Is the image of a faithful God not imaginable for you? Why or why not?

❖ Where have you seen God's faithfulness in your story?

❖ You may be going through a difficulty right now. Our mindsets get stronger by exercising gratitude and goodness. How can you implement Jeremiah's encouragement: "See the good, even if the good is not visible?" (I know it's hard to do when we are in the thick of difficulty but try this exercise right now in the space below because I know it will strengthen your mind.)

Day 27

God Sees So You Can
be a Woman at Ease

*She gave this name to the LORD who spoke to
her: "You are the God who sees me," for she
said, "I have now seen the One who sees me."
(Genesis 16:13)*

I saw him out of the corner of my eye as I was lifting my
20-pound weight at the gym. I sat on a bench and continued to watch in awe as he navigated his way around the
gym. This was not an ordinary young man. His white cane
revealed his identity, he was clearly a blind man.

As I sat there watching him maneuver around, I was
amazed at his ability to manipulate the weights. I wondered
about the thoughts and emotions that may have been running
through his mind because he wasn't able to see. I wondered if
he felt unseen by the world.

When we observe someone who is blind, we can't help but notice how their white cane becomes the stability factor in their lives. It gives them a sense of safety and security. I don't know about you, but I never want to take my eyesight for granted. Our eyesight gives us the ability to see our children's faces in their proudest moments, the majestic views of God's creation, and whatever is in front of us. Can you imagine seeing nothing but darkness? Think about how you feel when you are trying to walk in complete darkness, like when you try to navigate to the bathroom during the middle of the night. The dark creates a sense of insecurity, caution and even danger (from tripping or bumping into something), even in the familiarity of our own homes.

Likewise, when we don't feel seen in our arenas of life, we are left with similar emotions of insecurity, caution from impending danger, and insignificance. The married woman whose husband has not acknowledged her or tended to her needs in years can feel invisible. The single woman who has struggled to be seen and loved by someone can also feel as if she doesn't matter – to anyone. The woman whose dream was overlooked by another woman. The mom who is estranged by her adult children leaving and not keeping in touch. There exists a common thread in all our lives: the need to feel seen. If this need is not met, our human soul is squelched. There is nothing more painful than the feeling of being invisible, insignificant, unnoticed. I'm sure you, like me, have a story at some point in your life of struggling to feel seen and valued. Can we agree this struggle tends to be more real today, especially in our social media-dominated culture? As I ponder this, my soul contemplates this harsh reality – we are people desperate to be noticed, recognized, and applauded.

The Need to be Seen

Hagar is a woman in the Bible who struggled to be seen, just like you and me. She was an Egyptian maidservant to Abraham and Sarai, whose story is told in Genesis 16. God promised Abraham and Sarai He would build many nations through their descendants. However, this promise was unthinkable because Sarai was 65 years old – much too old to bear children. And after 10 years of simply growing older Sarai was frightened that the promise wouldn't be fulfilled so she took matters into her own hands. She told her husband to sleep with her maidservant, so through Hagar they could build a family. *What??!* No way would I have my husband sleep with our maid just to make our dream come true and build a family. But things were certainly different back in biblical days. Amidst the drama, Hagar learned she was pregnant, Sarai mistreated her, and Hagar chose to run away from her crazy mistress. (I pause in this story to wonder, *Did Hagar feel used for another person's agenda?* I would think so.) Hagar ran away to her familiar land of idolatry and false gods. But during her flight, God chased her down in a valley. She felt so unworthy of the chase, but then later felt favored (seen) by God's gracious visit. In the chase, God told Hagar to do something *extremely* difficult before He added favor. He told her, in essence, "Go back to Sarai and reconcile the relationship." I can imagine the nonsense of this request. How could Hagar do something like this after being mistreated? However, God was about to do something amazing with Hagar. He was going to increase *her* descendants, not just Abraham and Sarai's. Hagar would finally be a woman seen and regarded as significant through the blessing of many children (a symbol of value for biblical women). In her most desperate moment, we see Hagar chased by God. He *saw* her misery. Hagar, for the first time, gave God the name "El Roi" which is translated "The God who sees."

What is your story of not being seen? And are you running away to a place of familiarity because the pain is too much to bear? Could God be chasing you down, too? Are you noticing the chase and how are you responding, rejecting, or embracing it? God is chasing because He wants to assure you, He *sees* you. He notices the mistreatment or neglect. He hears your misery, He sees your broken dream. If you have run away to avoid more misery, I understand.

It hurts our egos when we have been used, mistreated, and devalued. In my own God chase, many times on my bedroom floor, I sensed God not only seeing my misery, but asking me to do the difficult thing. Like He did with Hagar, God calls us to be reconciled in relationship first, before He does something amazing. We never know the purpose behind the reconciliation, but it's often something more than we ever imagined. This, my friend warrants a claim in our life.... God is the God who *sees*.

> *God call us to be reconciled in relationship first, before He does something amazing.*

As Hagar finally felt noticed and recognized by God, she became a better tempered woman. Her behavior softened. She didn't live with bitterness and resentment any longer. Your story of struggle is impacted, when you realize "God sees." You, like Hagar, can live more at ease, not threatened by unfairness or concerned about your future, because you are confident that you are regarded, noticed, affirmed, and secured by your Heavenly Father who *sees*.

Being seen by God is *Better Than Espresso*

Realizing God Sees You

❖ Read the story of Hagar and Sarai in Genesis 16. Sarai became uneasy in the wait. She didn't believe God saw her desire to have children soon, so she took matters into her own hands. What is it that your heart desires, but doesn't yet have?

❖ Have you become uneasy in the wait? Yes or No

❖ Contemplate Hagar's response, "You are the God who sees me". Visualize your life in Hagar's. Thank God that even if you don't feel seen right now, he sees your misery and hears your heart's cry. He loves your faithfulness! Finish this thought: "You are the God who sees.....

Day 28

Pray Instead of Panic

I prayed to the LORD, and he answered me.
He freed me from all my fears.
(Psalm 34:4 NLT)

"What do you mean you can't come? How can you just cancel the day before?"

Panic began to overtake my emotions after this phone call. It was my son's second birthday. Since I was an event planner at the time, there was no shortage of fun and creativity for his birthday party. My son was in love with Thomas The Tank Engine, so we decided to be extravagant and hire a train company. I knew exactly where to find the entertainment and called the vendor for a booking. I called months in advance as a diligent party planner often does. I couldn't wait to see the adorable two-year-old toddlers wear their blue pin-striped conductor hats and blow their train whistles while riding the train up and down our street.

On the day before the party, I was running around town like any crazy birthday party mom finalizing all the goody bags and decorations. My cellphone rang, and I decided to pick it up even though I didn't have a second to talk. I couldn't believe what I just heard on the other end. It was my train vendor cancelling on my son's very important day. *Unbelievable!* How could this happen, especially the day before the event?

My oldest child knew mommy was upset. In that moment, I had a choice to make. Was I going to raise my voice and continue to panic, or was I going to take a deep breath and model a God-moment for my children? Honestly, I really felt like punching the window – I had no time for God in that moment! After taking a pause to regain my composure, I looked straight at my kids and said, "We have a problem, but instead of panicking, we are going to pray that God can help mommy find another train vendor for Cole's birthday party tomorrow." I pulled over to the side of the road and we bowed our heads, and prayed for God to help us find another train.

Have you ever encountered a similar stressful situation? I bet your blood pressure took a beating like mine. When situations arise out of our control, it's natural to panic, and get upset and even angry. Prayer is our most powerful arsenal to combat our panic and elevated emotions. When prayer becomes a priority, we begin to see its power.

> **When prayer becomes a priority, we begin to see its power.**

Prayer is An Act of Surrender

David, a prominent author of many of the Psalms, learned how prayer silences fear and panic. "Your rod and your staff, they comfort me" (Psalm 23:4). "The Lord is the stronghold of my life- of whom shall I be afraid"? (Psalm 27:1) Wow, we can learn so many lessons from David. Anytime there is an opportunity to silence my fear, panic, and worries, sign me up! David is noted in Scripture as a "man after God's heart" (1 Samuel 13:14). With this title, I am fairly confident prayer was one of his first priorities. I imagine a day never went by without meditative prayer. His life was probably a lot like yours and mine when it comes to our schedules. Well, then again, he was a king so his stress level was likely way more intense than ours. If I held a prominent position like him, you can be sure I would be face down on the carpet, seeking God for answers which are beyond my control and ability. Prayer provides a beautiful picture of surrender. That's why it's so important to God. He wants us to look to Him for answers, not ourselves, and certainly not to the world. When we look to Him, His gift of blessing minimizes our confusion and dismay.

My kids and I saw an example of that power after we surrendered our problem and determined to pray instead of panic. I happened to have a party magazine of vendors in my car and I called another train vendor. Can you believe with less than a 24- hour notice, the first train vendor I called after praying, was available? My little boy and all his friends were not going to miss the train and be left behind.

That experience taught me (and my kids) that God values our surrender and hears our prayers. God reveals His character in our prayer life. God showed me that He cared about my little boy. Now, you might be thinking at this moment that my story is such a trivial matter compared to what you're going through. You are probably right, but I don't want to discount God's desire to show His love and sovereignty over your life too. If you are in the midst of fear and panic, can I challenge you to pull over (if you're driving), stop, and place it under God's care. Further in the Psalm, it says "his ears are attentive to their cry" (verse 15). God is waiting, my friend, with focused eyes and all ears. No one else can give you this kind of attention. I'm excited to see how God's going to deliver as you trust Him with your prayer.

Our Heavenly Father frees us from our panic and fears. Prayer is the ultimate medicine for our panic and anxiety attacks. It may take time for you to become comfortable with the medicine of prayer, but as you begin to believe and take notice of God's divine sovereignty, your prayer life becomes less timid and more powerful.

Power of prayer is *Better Than Espresso*

Reflecting on Your Prayer Life

❖ What are your honest thoughts about prayer? Are you afraid of it? Do you resist it or doubt it? Or do you embrace it? Describe your thoughts here.

❖ Where have you seen the power of prayer in your life?

❖ If you are currently anxious, panicked, or fearful, fill in the blanks below and recite it every morning before you get out of bed.

> Lord, I am fearful and panicked about
>
> _____ (whatever is causing you fear and panic).
>
> Instead of feeling anxious about my situation, I give You permission to release it from my troubled soul. I trust You will take care of it and will set me free from:
>
> _____ (your strong-hold).

❖ Now, I bet you are feeling better already for giving your concern to God. His ears are attentive, and He listens to our prayers (1 Peter 3:12). Aren't you glad we have a God who is concerned about all our prayers, even the simplest ones like providing me a vendor for my son's birthday party? He cares about us that much!

Day 29

God Wants My Faith More than My Ultimatum

Gideon replied, "If now I have found favor in your eyes, give me a sign that it is really you talking to me."
(Judges 6:17)

I was ready to throw in the towel! I wasn't seeing any progress. All I saw was disappointment and defeat. How was I to keep going under those circumstances? Have you ever wanted to throw in the towel too?

I was wrestling with what to do about my non-profit ministry God had called me to lead the past several years. It ran strong for the first several years, and then suddenly, a gigantic shift. The parts that moved, were no longer moving. I saw this ministry starting to unfold before my very eyes. My tenacity was surely slipping away.

During this process of being ready to quit and move forward in a new direction, I received a couple of speaking inquiries from outside sources. I was hoping they would choose me but inside I was afraid, like how I feel sitting in the passenger seat while my teenager drives. *What if I crashed and totally messed it up?* I couldn't deal with another failure and disappointment. I remember the moment well, my face positioned to the floor, crying and pleading with God.

"God, I don't see You. I don't hear You!"

I was exhausted in my striving. I didn't want to do ministry any longer. I wanted to illuminate the "Closed" sign on my business and pursue a *real* job where I could receive a paycheck and hibernate in the background. I was so desperate, so I gave God an ultimatum:

If one of these speaking requests is a solid yes, then it's a sign to keep going. If not, I'll see it as a sign to go in a new direction.

This was a bold move for me. I was taught to pray, trust, and have more faith. I had never given God an ultimatum and I didn't know if it was the right thing to do. But, I was desperate for an answer. And God answered. He *always* does. Surprisingly, from the two requests, the larger venue chose me. I certainly didn't feel qualified, but I knew this was my assignment from God and I had to walk in obedience.

Gideon's Ultimatum

Gideon also gave God an ultimatum. He was chosen to fight the Midianites (people who were against the Israelites in Old Testament times). He kept making excuses to God why he was not the right person for the job. He needed a sign to move forward. God gave him his first sign, but it wasn't convincing enough for Gideon; he needed more. Finally, after arguing with God, Gideon presented God with an ultimatum.

> *"'If you will save Israel by my hand as you have promised – look, I will place a wool fleece on the threshing floor. If there is dew only on the fleece and all the ground is dry, then I will know that you will save Israel by my hand, as you said.' And that is what happened. Gideon rose early the next day; he squeezed the fleece and wrung out the dew – a bowlful of water. Then Gideon said to God, 'Do not be angry with me. Let me make just one more request. Allow me one more test with the fleece. This time make the fleece dry and the ground covered with dew.' That night God did so. Only the fleece was dry; all the ground was covered with dew"* (Judges 6: 38-40).

Gideon was a man of God who just lacked a little faith. His fleece represented an "immature faith" because as you read the prior verses, God had already given him a sign that "He's the guy." But Gideon needed more assurance. His small faith reminds me of mine at times – and perhaps yours, too? God prefers to meet us in our raw faith as opposed to our ultimatums (demanding signs). However, I believe sometimes there are moments where we are desperate for a visible sign because our fear has taken over. This was certainly my case. But I learned in my expe-

> **Replace frustration with truth and trust.**

rience that God desires for me to replace my frustration with truth and trust. As a parent, I know my kids need an extra push and assurance to help them feel more secure when uncertainty strikes. God works in a similar fashion. His heart is to assure me that *He sees me.* He wants to give me every opportunity to grow in my trust toward Him. His Word is very clear to not put God to the test (Mathew 4:7). However, if we are truly seeking the heart of God and not our own selfish desires, I believe He understands when we just need a little more evidence. He's aware of our immature faith and gives us second chances to notice Him again.

If you are in a desperate place, seeking a sign and answer, get on your knees and spill out your heart to God. If fear is causing you to be paralyzed, admit it, and then present to God your ultimatum. Our response thereafter should be thanking Him for how He is going to answer, and then moving into greater faith. After all, God is using your ultimatum to grow your faith, so your need won't be as strong for a sign or ultimatum in the future.

Sovereign faith is *Better Than Espresso*

Reflecting on Your Need for an Ultimatum

❖ Are you in a situation where you are ready to throw in the towel? Why do you feel this way? Record your thoughts below.

❖ Considering Gideon's story, do you think it is right or wrong to give God an ultimatum? Yes or No
Explain the reason for your answer.

❖ Scripture tells us "Trust in him at all times... pour out your hearts to him, for God is our refuge." (Psalm 62:8) Why is it difficult to trust God with our life assignments?

❖ It is my prayer that God will show Himself strong on your behalf, as your safe refuge while you wait upon Him for the answer you seek.

Day 30

Peace is Present without Perfection, Performance, and People Pleasing

Am I now trying to win the approval of human beings, or of God? Or am I trying to please people? If I were still trying to please people, I would not be a servant of Christ.
(Galatians 1:10)

Think back to your school days. How did you feel when you had to give a presentation to the class? Are you the type of person who enjoyed standing on stage capturing the crowd's attention? If not, I assume your hands got clammy, your heart palpitated, and your forehead dripped with sweat when you needed to speak in front of others.

I was the student who preferred oral presentations over taking written tests. Honestly, I preferred using my voice, rather than a pencil and paper.

Yet, no matter how much I enjoyed presenting (and performing), I still got nervous. *What if I didn't articulate my words correctly? Would I appear stupid and incompetent among my peers?* No wonder public speaking is one of people's greatest fears. I remember one instance when I was on stage speaking, and my brain was just not functioning like it should. I fumbled over all my words, like a football player fumbling a key play. I felt like a complete idiot. This was my chance to shine with my natural energy and charisma, impress the crowd, and appeal to the leader who assigned me such a great privilege. I knew I had disappointed this person and the shame of "not being eloquent enough" struck in my inner core. I walked off the stage with my head low, embarrassed by my failed performance. All I could think about was how I felt like a fool and I would never be given this opportunity to speak again. Clearly, I was stuck in the expectation of perfect performance and striving for others' approval. My inner critic waged war with my mind and emotions. I replayed my mess-up numerous times leaving me insecure and in turmoil.

Do you, too, at times experience an unhealthy need to be perfect, perform for approval, or people please for acceptance? If so, do you notice how you are being robbed of peace, joy, and self-compassion?

Perfection is that inner critic that compares you to others as you stroll through your social media feeds. *Why aren't you as perfect as that woman who posts pictures of her beautiful magnolia home and her family posed in front of the white picket fence? Why can't you be the mom who posts pics of your academically gifted child who just got accepted into a prestigious college? Why can't you make progress like your friend who just lost 20 pounds and posed for a selfie in her tight designer jeans and sleeveless top?* My, how social media has warped our ideas into feeling the need to look perfect! A struggle with performance is feeling accepted and approved only by what you achieve. (I am being transparent, this is my downfall.) The problem with performance is that it will continue to elude you and eventually exhaust you. I am rarely my best if I am so consumed with how I look, how I performed, and how I am impressing those around me. And when I am not my best, I get into the rut of self-condemnation rather than being kind to myself. If you tend to be a people pleaser like me, you probably don't like conflict in your relationships. Your friend asks you a favor and you are always saying yes because you don't want to disappoint her, even though it's inconvenient. Repeatedly saying yes may be an indication that you struggle with establishing boundaries. Setting boundaries is a struggle because avoiding conflict is easier for you and the need to be accepted is more important. These 3 P's (perfection, performance, people pleasing) can really disrupt our personal peace, right?

Looking to God for Approval

As Galatians 1:10 says, if we are trying to win the approval of others, it's difficult to be our best us. Being a servant of Christ means presenting our best to the world. It means being comfortable in who God designed us to be. Our best allows us to serve and love others well. Constantly seeking approval from others is similiar to living like a chameleon – relying on others to confirm "we are good enough". Here's the truth. People will fail us, God will not. It's so difficult to be a person of inner peace when we are constantly practicing the 3 P's in order to please the world. Why is it such a fight to do away with perfectionism, performance, and people pleasing?

Maybe it's because we have a need to appear strong, attractive, independent, capable and worthy. When we feel anything less than that, we can tend to feel unloved and unaccepted.

Paul, an apostle of Christ, understood the temptation to please others more than God. Before he knew God, he was a religious zealot. He was all about showing off his words, knowledge, and academic life to those he regarded as less skilled and worthy as himself. He used his intellect to persuade and argue with others. He probably gained applause and sentiment for his intellectual ability. Can you imagine his demeanor? He must have been so conceited, thinking *Men are impressed by me, I perform like no other. Applaud and notice me, for I am a man full of knowledge and wisdom.* But after his spiritual transformation, he learned that

> *Allegiance to God settles our soul more than allegiance to people.*

allegiance to God settled his soul more than allegiance to people. I can imagine how humbling this was for Paul, a man who seemed to know it all and be in total control of his life. As Paul's relationship with God grew, I think he understood how gaining approval from others deters us from sharing our authentic selves with the world.

Because of my own struggle with the three P's, I have had to do more stripping, so God can do the settling. The less attention I give to the 3 P's, the more peace I exude with who I am. As I surrender this struggle, I notice a huge difference. Recently, I had a speaking engagement and my authentic self was evolving rather than my performing self. I felt so natural, so peaceful. I didn't need to impress the audience with my performance because God was settling my formerly unsettled soul. I stepped off the stage peaceful and confident, assured that I acted as a servant of Christ instead of a performer for people. What a huge difference it makes when our lives are shaped more like servants than performers. Peace is more present. You won't be too consumed with pleasing your boss or overly worried if your work is good enough. Your work will flow naturally and from a place of authentic impact and influence. Your life becomes a magnet – people want to know you, follow you, be influenced by you because of your settled assurance of pleasing God, not others. You won't be fighting that voice in your head that says, *I will never measure up.* Instead, you will believe more in what your Maker says, than what mankind says. These are the signs of a woman who is at *peace* because she has removed the barriers of perfection, performance, and people pleasing.

Inner peace is *Better Than Espresso*

Reflecting the Need to be Perfect, Perform, and People Please

❖ If you struggle with perfectionism, you are probably your own worst critic. Take a moment and reflect on the areas in your life where you meet the most self-criticism. Be honest with yourself and write them down here.

❖ How can you release yourself from judgment and turn each criticism toward something good?

❖ People pleasers have a difficult time setting boundaries and saying "no" because they either don't like conflict or they need approval from others. Is there a situation right now in which you need to set a boundary? Identify it and use this space to write down how you can articulate your boundary.

❖ God desires us to have an inner peace. His word says, "peace I give you... not like the world. Let your heart not be troubled" (John 14:27). Our hearts can easily be troubled when we are consumed with perfection, performance, and people pleasing. I pray for both of us that God can help refine our 3 P's. I'm cheering us on ,inner peace is on its way for you and me!

A PARTING
ENCOURAGEMENT

Congratulations, you did it! You completed these 30 days and it's been such a pleasure to walk alongside you. I hope this devotional has encouraged your heart, quenched your soul, and drawn you closer to the God who adores you. There is nothing better than experiencing freedom from the distorted thoughts that control our mind, and waking up ready with a "winning mindset." Moving forward with more confidence and a God-empowered faith is truly *Better Than Espresso* (even for the coffee maniac like myself). If you feel more equipped to renew your minds, and combat the lies that shape your thoughts, then you truly have achieved what I had hoped and prayed this book would accomplish.

I encourage you to remember what you've learned by applying some of my Sticky Quote Mirror Decals (with your favorite confidence-building quotes) in a place where you can read, recite and repeat them often. You can find them on my website at this address: https://juliepearson.org/shop/.

Finally, I would love to hear how this book has helped you and how you intend to pass on what you've learned to others. Please contact me at my email address:Julie@juliepearson.org or leave a note on my website: www.Juliepearson.org . If you enjoyed the book, kindly write a review and share the Amazon link with your friends. I hope to stay in touch. Spending these past 30 days with you has been *Better Than Espresso...*

Your Cheerleader,

Julie

LET'S BE FRIENDS
FOLLOW ME HERE:

Facebook: @juliepearsonblog
Instagram: @juliepearson68
Linked In: Julie Pearson
https://www.linkedin.com/in/julie-pearson-a54aa813/

#Betterthanespresso

Notes

Day 7: Losing Makes Me Better

1. Michael Jordan's quote can be found at: https://www.entrepreneur.com/article/325840, January 2019.

Day 20: Training Prepares Me for the Win

1. Crystal Evans Hurts, *Show Up for Your Life* (Zondervan: Grand Rapids, Michigan: 2018).

Acknowledgments

Thank you to these individuals for supporting me in my journey.

To my amazing husband, Cannon: Thank you for being my perfect partner. Your love is more than I can speak. Thank you for your sacrifice of making sure the kids were well fed the nights my head was buried in my words. Thank you for your encouragement, and always being willing to read and edit my work. Your belief helped me persevere. I love you more than anything!

To my precious children (Brianna, Cole, Ashlyn): Thank you for my biggest gift; being my amazing children. Thank you for your love and support. I am thankful for your patience and giving mom space to finalize her book during the "stay home" pandemic. I love you "all the way to the moon and back." Thank you to my dog, Bennett, who kept me company as I clicked away.

To Mom and Dad: I am one fortunate daughter to have such loving parents. Thank you for your sacrificial love, always lending a hand when I need you. Thank you for all your support and never allowing me to give up. Thank you for your value of family and providing me a strong foundation of faith. I love you!

To my Extended Family: Thank you all for loving me through the good and hard times. I am proud to call you my family (the best Italian family). Special thanks to Aunt Rose Ann for supporting my ministry and always cheering me on. Special thanks to Leanna for helping me launch my book sales at one of my events.

To my Writing Coach and Editor: Thank you Cindi McMenamin for your amazing skill of editing and helping me express myself better. Thank you for the potential you saw in my writing skills. I am forever grateful for your graceful coaching.

To my best friends: Thank you Lisa and Julia for the long-time friendship. Words can't explain how blessed I am to have you in my life. You two are the sisters I never had. Thank you for cheering me on and your encouragement.

To my Tribe: Thank you for supporting me during the initial stages of writing this book. Thank you Lou, Stacie, Julia, Denise, Jennifer P, Jennifer G, Kristina, and Lisa for the long night wrestling through the title. You girls did a fantastic job! Thank you for your time and sacrifice.

To my Barnabas's: Thank you Brandi for your partnership in ministry. Thank you for opening my eyes to "Stand in my God-given power." Thank you Danae for the numerous coffee dates, cheering each other, and your valuable feedback. Thank you Melody for your friendship and support in ministry. I always enjoyed our lunch dates.

Special Mentions: Thank you Michelle, Rachel, and Kim for pioneering my pre-launch and working my book table at one of my events. Thank you, Heather, for your cheerleading spirit. Thank you to my close circle of friends (Lou, Kim, Stacie, Small Group) for the support and the fun memories we have shared.

ABOUT THE AUTHOR

Julie Pearson has a passion to help women become restored in the difficult areas of life, so they can be revived in the new! She motivates, inspires, and cheers women in all seasons of life to be the "very best woman" God has created her to be. She empowers moms, singles, and married women to live a life of great faith instead of fear. She has more than 15 years experience speaking at various women's events including MOPS, women's retreats, outreach conferences, and Bible study groups. You can also find Julie on your favorite podcast platform. *Revive Podcast with Julie Pearson* is a place to hear inspiring testimonies how God **Restored** women and men and now are living a life of Revival.

Along with writing and speaking, she is the Founder of her Non-Profit Ministry, Revival 4 Women, focused on building authentic community to refresh, renew, and restore women. Her organization sponsors a local non-profit, Thrive Single Moms, that donates resources for single moms. Julie understands the life demands on single moms and is donating 15% of her book sales to Thrive Single Moms. Thank you for helping a single mom thrive through your book purchase. www.thrivesinglemoms.org.

Check out the next few pages, samples of the Sticky Quote Mirror Decals. If you need a boost of faith and confidence, my hope is that you will stick these non-adhesive mirror decals on your morning mirror for a positive message first thing in the morning. You can purchase here:

https://juliepearson.org/shop/

Comparison is a
TRAP
It Can Kill My
CONFIDENCE©

JuliePearson.org

Galatians 6:4-5

God

Doesn't Fail Me,

He

Goes Before Me ©

JuliePearson.org   Deuteronomy 31:8

Life Will Knock Me

Down

But I Have a Choice to

Get Back Up

JuliePearson.org   Joshua 1:9 ©

Just Start
and
Don't Worry
About
Being Great.

JuliePearson.org

Job 8:7

Changing My *Perspective*

Changes My *Posture*©

JuliePearson.org

Romans 12:2

Attach Value to My
"Who,"

♥ ♥ ♥

Not My
"Do."

JuliePearson.org

Jeremiah 1:5

Your daily Sticky Quotes

Day 1: There is Purpose in My Pause
Day 2: God Is My Strength, He is Bigger Than My Failure
Day 3: Worry Exhausts, Wisdom Energizes
Day 4: Fear Asks: What if it Doesn't Work? Faith Asks: What if it Does Work?
Day 5: Life Will Knock Me Down, But I Have a Choice to Get Back up
Day 6: Comparison is a Trap, it Can Kill My Confidence
Day 7: Losing Makes Me Better
Day 8: My Confidence Grows Stronger as God Delivers
Day 9: Just Start and Don't Worry About Being Great
Day 10: Heal From Rejection or it will Become an Infection
Day 11: God Doesn't Fail Me, He Goes Before Me
Day 12: I'm Learning to Laugh at Myself, Not Shame Myself
Day 13: Staying in My Past Paralyzes My Present
Day 14: My Hard Moments Humble Me, Not Harm Me
Day 15: My Broken Pieces Prepare Me for a Breakthrough
Day 16: Don't Resist My Re-route, Embrace it
Day 17: I'll Let Go of My Ideal and Let God Lead
Day 18: Being Comfortable with Who I am Allows Me to Be Certain of Where I Am Going
Day 19: God Finds Me When I Am Lost
Day 20: Training Prepares Me for the Win
Day 21: Changing My Perspective Changes My Posture
Day 22: Attach Value to My "Who", Not My "Do"
Day 23: Progress Comes When I Plug into My God-Given Power

Day 24: My Hacker Intrudes, But My God Renews
Day 25: Filter Old Thoughts to Make Room for the New
Day 26: God's Not Finished with Me Yet
Day 27: God Sees, So You Can Be a Woman At Ease
Day 28: Pray Instead of Panic
Day 29: God Wants My Faith More than My Ultimatum
Day 30: Peace is Present without Perfection, Performance, and People Pleasing

Reflect on Your Daily Sticky Quotes From Your Morning Mirror.
Order Mirror Decals Here:
https://juliepearson.org/shop/

Made in the USA
Monee, IL
07 November 2020

46969334R00118